GOD'S DESIGN® FOR HEAV

MW00713032

TEACHER
SUPPLEMENT

1:1

answersingenesis

Petersburg, Kentucky, USA

ANSWERS IN GENESIS **SCIENCE** BY DEBBIE & RICHARD LAWRENCE

God's Design® for Heaven & Earth Teacher Supplement

© 2008 by Debbie & Richard Lawrence

No part of this book may be reproduced in any form or by any means without written permission from the author and publisher other than: (1) the specific pages within the book that are designed for single family/classroom use, and (2) as brief quotations quoted in a review.

Published by Answers in Genesis, 2800 Bullittsburg Church Rd., Petersburg KY 41080

You may contact the authors at (970) 686-5744.
ISBN: 1-60092-229-5

Cover design & layout: Diane King
Editors: Lori Jaworski, Gary Vaterlaus

All scripture quotations are taken from the New King James Version. Copyright 1982 by Thomas Nelson, Inc. Used by permission. All rights reserved.

The publisher and authors have made every reasonable effort to ensure that the activities recommended in this book are safe when performed as instructed but assume no responsibility for any damage caused or sustained while conducting the experiments and activities. It is the parents', guardians', and/or teachers' responsibility to supervise all recommended activities.

Printed in China.

www.answersingenesis.org   www.godsdesignscience.com

TABLE OF CONTENTS

TEACHER INTRODUCTION

WELCOME TO GOD'S DESIGN® FOR HEAVEN & EARTH

God's Design for Heaven and Earth is a series that has been designed for use in teaching earth science to elementary and middle school students. It is divided into three books: *Our Universe, Our Planet Earth,* and *Our Weather and Water.* Each book has 35 lessons including a final project that ties all of the lessons together.

In addition to the lessons, special features in each book include biographical information on interesting people as well as fun facts to make the subject more fun.

Although this is a complete curriculum, the information included here is just a beginning, so please feel free to add to each lesson as you see fit. A resource guide is included in the appendices to help you find additional information and resources. A list of supplies needed is included at the beginning of each lesson, while a master list of all supplies needed for the entire series can be found in the appendices.

Answer keys for all review questions, worksheets, quizzes, and the final exam are included here. Reproducible student worksheets and tests may be found on the supplementary CD-Rom for easy printing. Please contact Answers in Genesis if you wish to purchase a printed version of all the student materials, or go to www.AnswersBookstore.com.

If you wish to get through the *Heaven and Earth* series in one year, plan on covering approximately three lessons per week. The time required for each lesson varies depending on how much additional information you include, but plan on 20 minutes per lesson for beginners (grades 1–2) and 40 to 45 minutes for grades 3–8.

Quizzes may be given at the conclusion of each unit and the final exam may be given after lesson 34.

If you wish to cover the material in more depth, you may add additional information and take a longer period of time to cover all the material, or you could choose to do only one or two of the books in the series as a unit study.

WHY TEACH EARTH SCIENCE?

It is not uncommon to question the need to teach children hands-on science in elementary or middle school. We could argue that the knowledge gained in science will be needed later in life in order for children to be more productive and well-rounded adults. We could argue that teaching children science also teaches them logical and inductive thinking and reasoning skills, which are tools they will need to be more successful. We could argue that science is a necessity in this technological world in which we live. While all of these arguments are true, not one of them is the main reason that we should teach our children science. The most important reason to teach science in elementary school is to give children an understanding that God is our Creator, and the Bible can be trusted. Teaching science from a creation perspective is one of the best ways to reinforce our children's faith in God and to help them counter the evolutionary propaganda they face every day.

God is the Master Creator of everything. His handiwork is all around us. Our great Creator put in place all of the laws of physics, biology, and chemistry. These laws were put here for us to see His wisdom and power. In science, we see the hand of God at work more than in any other subject. Romans 1:20 says, "For since the creation of the world His invisible attributes are clearly seen, being understood by the things that are made, even His eternal power and Godhead, so that they [men] are without excuse." We need to help our children see God as Creator of the world around them so they will be able to recognize God and follow Him.

The study of earth science helps us to understand and appreciate this amazing world God gave us. Studying the processes that shape the earth, and exploring the origins of the earth and the universe often bring us into direct conflict with evolutionary theories. This is why it is so critical to teach our children the truth of the Bible, how to evaluate the evidence, how to distinguish fact from theory, and to realize that the evidence, rightly interpreted, supports biblical creation not evolution.

It's fun to teach earth science! It's interesting too. Rocks, weather, and stars are all around us. Children naturally collect rocks and gaze at the stars. You just need to direct their curiosity.

Finally, teaching earth science is easy. It's where you live. You won't have to try to find strange materials for experiments or do dangerous things to learn about the earth.

HOW DO I TEACH SCIENCE?

In order to teach any subject you need to understand how people learn. People learn in different ways. Most people, and children in particular, have a dominant or preferred learning style in which they absorb and retain information more easily.

If a student's dominant style is:

AUDITORY
He needs not only to hear the information but he needs to hear himself say it. This child needs oral presentation as well as oral drill and repetition.

VISUAL
She needs things she can see. This child responds well to flashcards, pictures, charts, models, etc.

KINESTHETIC
he needs active participation. This child remembers best through games, hands-on activities, experiments, and field trips.

Also, some people are more relational while others are more analytical. The relational student needs to know why this subject is important, and how it will affect him personally. The analytical student, however, wants just the facts.

If you are trying to teach more than one student, you will probably have to deal with more than one learning style. Therefore, you need to present your lessons in several different ways so that each student can grasp and retain the information.

GRADES 1–2

Because *God's Design Science* books are designed to be used with students in grades 1–8, each lesson has been divided into three sections. The "Beginner" section is for students in grades 1–2. This part contains a read-aloud section explaining the material for that lesson followed by a few questions to make sure that the students understand what they just heard. We recommend that you do the hands-on activity in the blue box in the main part of the lesson to help your students see and understand the concepts.

GRADES 3–8

The second part of each lesson should be completed by all upper elementary and junior high students. This is the main part of the lesson containing a reading section, a hands-on activity that reinforces the ideas in the reading section (blue box), and a review section that provides review questions and application questions (red box).

GRADES 6–8

Finally, for middle school/junior high age students, we provide a "Challenge" section that contains more challenging material as well as additional activities and projects for older students (green box).

We have included periodic biographies to help your students appreciate the great men and women who have gone before us in the field of science.

We suggest a threefold approach to each lesson:

INTRODUCE THE TOPIC

We give a brief description of the facts. Frequently you will want to add more information than the essentials given in this book. In addition to reading this section aloud (or having older children read it on their own), you may wish to do one or more of the following:

- Read a related book with your students.
- Write things down to help your visual learners.
- Give some history of the subject. We provide some historical sketches to help you, but you may want to add more.
- Ask questions to get your students thinking about the subject.

MAKE OBSERVATIONS AND DO EXPERIMENTS

- Hands-on projects are suggested for each lesson. This part of each lesson may require help from the teacher.
- Have your students perform the activity by themselves whenever possible.

REVIEW

- The "What did we learn?" section has review questions.
- The "Taking it further" section encourages students to
  - Draw conclusions
  - Make applications of what was learned
  - Add extended information to what was covered in the lesson
- The "FUN FACT" section adds fun or interesting information.

By teaching all three parts of the lesson, you will be presenting the material in a way that children with any learning style can both relate to and remember.

Also, this approach relates directly to the scientific method and will help your students think more scientifically. The *scientific method* is just a way to examine a subject logically and learn from it. Briefly, the steps of the scientific method are:

1. Learn about a topic.

2. Ask a question.

3. Make a hypothesis (a good guess).

4. Design an experiment to test your hypothesis.

5. Observe the experiment and collect data.

6. Draw conclusions. (Does the data support your hypothesis?)

Note: It's okay to have a "wrong hypothesis." That's how we learn. Be sure to help your students understand why they sometimes get a different result than expected.

Our lessons will help your students begin to approach problems in a logical, scientific way.

HOW DO I TEACH CREATION VS. EVOLUTION?

We are constantly bombarded by evolutionary ideas about the earth in books, movies, museums, and even commercials. These raise many questions: What is the big bang? How old is the earth? Do fossils show evolution to be true? Was there really a worldwide flood? When did dinosaurs live? Was there an ice age? How can we teach our children the truth about the origins of the earth? The Bible answers these questions and this book accepts the historical accuracy of the Bible as written. We believe this is the only way we can teach our children to trust that everything God says is true.

There are five common views of the origins of life and the age of the earth:

Historical biblical account	Progressive creation	Gap theory	Theistic evolution	Naturalistic evolution
Each day of creation in Genesis is a normal day of about 24 hours in length, in which God created everything that exists. The earth is only thousands of years old, as determined by the genealogies in the Bible.	The idea that God created various creatures to replace other creatures that died out over millions of years. Each of the days in Genesis represents a long period of time (day-age view) and the earth is billions of years old.	The idea that there was a long, long time between what happened in Genesis 1:1 and what happened in Genesis 1:2. During this time, the "fossil record" was supposed to have formed, and millions of years of earth history supposedly passed.	The idea that God used the process of evolution over millions of years (involving struggle and death) to bring about what we see today.	The view that there is no God and evolution of all life forms happened by purely naturalistic processes over billions of years. Ken Ham et al., *The Answers Book*, (El Cajon: Master Books, 2000), 33–76.

Any theory that tries to combine the evolutionary time frame with creation presupposes that death entered the world before Adam sinned, which contradicts what God has said in His Word. The view that the earth (and its "fossil record") is hundreds of millions of years old damages the gospel message. God's completed creation was "very good" at the end of the sixth day (Genesis 1:31). Death entered this perfect paradise *after* Adam disobeyed God's command. It was the punishment for Adam's sin (Genesis 2:16–17, 3:19; Romans 5:12–19). Thorns appeared when God cursed the ground because of Adam's sin (Genesis 3:18).

The first animal death occurred when God killed at least one animal, shedding its blood, to make clothes for Adam and Eve (Genesis 3:21). If the earth's "fossil record" (filled with death, disease, and thorns) formed over millions of years before Adam appeared (and before he sinned), then death no longer would be the penalty for sin. Death, the "last enemy" (1 Corinthians 15:26), diseases (such as cancer), and thorns would instead be part of the original creation that God labeled "very good." No, it is clear that the "fossil record" formed some time *after* Adam sinned—not many millions of years before. Most fossils were formed as a result of the worldwide Genesis Flood.

When viewed from a biblical perspective, the scientific evidence clearly supports a recent creation by God, and not naturalistic evolution and millions of years. The volume of evidence supporting the biblical creation account is substantial and cannot be adequately covered in this book. If you would like more information on this topic, please see the resource guide in Appendix A. To help get you started, just a few examples of evidence supporting biblical creation are given below:

Evolutionary Myth: The earth is 4.6 billion years old.

The Truth: Many processes observed today point to a young earth of only a few thousand years. The rate at which the earth's magnetic field is decaying suggests the earth must be less than 10,000 years old. The rate of population growth and the recent emergence of civilization suggests only a few thousand years of human population. And, at the current rate of accumulation, the amount of mud on the sea floor should be many kilometers thick if the earth were billions of years old. However, the average depth of all the mud in the whole ocean is less than 400 meters, giving a maximum age for the earth of not more than 12 million years. All this and more indicates an earth much younger than 4.6 billion years.

John D. Morris, Ph.D., *The Young Earth* (Colorado Springs: Creation Life Publishers, 1994), 70–71, 83–90. See also: "Young age of the earth and universe" at www.answersingenesis.org/go/young.

Evolutionary Myth: The universe formed from the big bang.

The Truth: There are many problems with this theory. It does not explain where the initial material came from. It cannot explain what caused that material to fly apart in the first place. And nothing in physics indicates what would make the particles begin to stick together instead of flying off into space forever. The big bang theory contradicts many scientific laws. Because of these problems, some scientists have abandoned the big bang and are attempting to develop new theories to explain the origin of the universe.

Alex Williams & John Hartnett, Ph.D., *Dismantling the Big Bang* (Master Books, 2005). See also: "What are some of the problems with the 'big bang' hypothesis?" www.answersingenesis.org/go/big-bang.

Evolutionary Myth: Fossils prove evolution.

The Truth: While Darwin predicted that the fossil record would show numerous transitional fossils, even more than 145 years later, all we have are a handful of disputable examples. For example, there are no fossils showing something that is part way between a dinosaur and a bird. Fossils show that a snail has always been a snail; a squid has always been a squid. God created each animal to reproduce after its kind (Genesis 1:20–25).

Evolutionary Myth: There is not enough water for a worldwide flood.

The Truth: Prior to the Flood, just as today, much of the water was stored beneath the surface of the earth. In addition, Genesis 1 states that the water below was separated from the water above, indicating that the atmosphere may have contained a great deal more water than it does today. Also, it is likely that before the Flood the mountains were not as high as they are today, but that the mountains rose and the valleys sank *after* the Flood began, as Psalm 104:6–9 suggests. At the beginning of the Flood, the fountains of the deep burst forth and it rained for 40 days and nights. This could have provided more than enough water to flood the entire earth. Indeed, if the entire earth's surface were leveled by smoothing out the topography of not only the land surface but also the rock surface on the ocean floor, the waters of the present-day oceans would cover the earth's surface to a depth of 1.7 miles (2.7 kilometers). Fossils have been found on the highest mountain peaks around the world showing that the waters of the Flood did indeed cover the entire earth.

Ken Ham et al., *The Answers Book*, (Master Books, 2000), 149–158.

Evolutionary Myth: Slow climate changes over time have resulted in multiple ice ages.

The Truth: There is widespread evidence of glaciers in many parts of the world indicating one ice age. Evolutionists find the cause of the Ice Age a mystery. Obviously, the climate would need to be colder. But global cooling by itself is not enough, because then there would be less evaporation, so less snow. How is it possible to have both a cold climate and lots of evaporation? The Ice Age was most likely an aftermath of Noah's Flood. When "all the fountains of the great deep" broke up, much hot water and lava would have poured directly into the oceans. This would have warmed the oceans, increasing evaporation. At the same time, much volcanic ash in the air after the Flood would have blocked out much sunlight, cooling the land. So the Flood would have produced the necessary combination of increased evaporation from the warmed oceans and cool continental climate from the volcanic ash in the air. This would have resulted in increased snowfall over the continents. With the snow falling faster than it melted, ice sheets would have built up. The Ice Age probably lasted less than 700 years.

Michael Oard, *Frozen in Time*, Master Books, 2004. See also www.answersingenesis.org/go/ice-age

Evolutionary Myth: Thousands of random changes over millions of years resulted in the earth we see today.

The Truth: The second law of thermodynamics describes how any system tends toward a state of zero entropy or disorder. We observe how everything around us becomes less organized and loses energy. The changes required for the formation of the universe, the planet earth and life, all from disorder, run counter to the physical laws we see at work today. There is no known mechanism to harness the raw energy of the universe and generate the specified complexity we see all around us.

John D. Morris, Ph.D., *The Young Earth*, (Colorado Springs: Creation Life Publishers, 1994), 43. See also www.answersin-genesis.org/go/thermodynamics.

Despite the claims of many scientists, if you examine the evidence objectively, it is obvious that evolution and millions of years have not been proven. You can be confident that if you teach that what the Bible says is true, you won't go wrong. Instill in your student a confidence in the truth of the Bible in all areas. If scientific thought seems to contradict the Bible, realize that scientists often make mistakes, but God does not lie. At one time scientists believed that the earth was the center of the universe, that living things could spring from non-living things, and that blood-letting was good for the body. All of these were believed to be scientific facts but have since been disproved, but the Word of God remains true. If we use modern "science" to interpret the Bible, what will happen to our faith in God's Word when scientists change their theories yet again?

INTEGRATING THE SEVEN C'S INTO YOUR CURRICULUM

Throughout the *God's Design® for Science* series you will see icons that represent the Seven C's of History. The Seven C's is a framework in which all of history, and the future to come, can be placed. As we go through our daily routines we may not understand how the details of life connect with the truth that we find in the Bible. This is also the case for students. When discussing the importance of the Bible you may find yourself telling students that the Bible is relevant in everyday activities. But how do we help the younger generation see that? The Seven C's are intended to help.

The Seven C's can be used to develop a biblical worldview in students, young or old. Much more than entertaining stories and religious teachings, the Bible has real connections to our everyday life. It may be hard, at first, to see how many connections there are, but with practice ,the daily relevance of God's Word will come alive. Let's look at the Seven C's of History and how each can be connected to what the students are learning.

CREATION

God perfectly created the heavens, the earth, and all that is in them in six normal-length days around 6,000 years ago.

This teaching is foundational to a biblical worldview and can be put into the context of any subject. In science, the amazing design that we see in nature—whether in the veins of a leaf or the complexity of your hand—is all the handiwork of God. Virtually all of the lessons in *God's Design for Science* can be related to God's creation of the heavens and earth.

Other contexts include:

Natural laws—any discussion of a law of nature naturally leads to God's creative power.

DNA and information—the information in every living thing was created by God's supreme intelligence.

Mathematics—the laws of mathematics reflect the order of the Creator.

Biological diversity—the distinct kinds of animals that we see were created during the Creation Week, not as products of evolution.

Art—the creativity of man is demonstrated through various art forms.

History—all time scales can be compared to the biblical time scale extending back about 6,000 years.

Ecology—God has called mankind to act as stewards over His creation.

CORRUPTION

After God completed His perfect creation, Adam disobeyed God by eating the forbidden fruit. As a result, sin and death entered the world, and the world has been in decay since that time. This point is evident throughout the world that we live in. The struggle for survival in animals, the death of loved ones, and the violence all around us are all examples of the corrupting influence of sin.

Other contexts include:

Genetics—the mutations that lead to diseases, cancer, and variation within populations are the result of corruption.

Biological relationships—predators and parasites result from corruption.

History—wars and struggles between mankind, exemplified in the account of Cain and Abel, are a result of sin.

CATASTROPHE

God was grieved by the wickedness of mankind and judged this wickedness with a global Flood. The Flood covered the entire surface of the earth and killed all air-breathing creatures that were not aboard the Ark. The eight people and the animals aboard the Ark replenished the earth after God delivered them from the catastrophe.

The catastrophe described in the Bible would naturally leave behind much evidence. The studies of geology and of the biological diversity of animals on the planet are two of the most obvious applications of this event. Much of scientific understanding is based on how a scientist views the events of the Genesis Flood.

Other contexts include:

Biological diversity—all of the birds, mammals, and other air-breathing animals have populated the earth from the original kinds which left the Ark.

Geology—the layers of sedimentary rock seen in roadcuts, canyons, and other geologic features are testaments to the global Flood.

Geography—features like mountains, valleys, and plains were formed as the floodwaters receded.

Physics—rainbows are a perennial sign of God's faithfulness and His pledge to never flood the entire earth again.

Fossils—Most fossils are a result of the Flood rapidly burying plants and animals.

Plate tectonics—the rapid movement of the earth's plates likely accompanied the Flood.

Global warming/Ice Age—both of these items are likely a result of the activity of the Flood. The warming we are experiencing today has been present since the peak of the Ice Age (with variations over time).

CONFUSION

God commanded Noah and his descendants to spread across the earth. The refusal to obey this command and the building of the tower at Babel caused God to judge this sin. The common language of the people was confused and they spread across the globe as groups with a common language. All people are truly of "one blood" as descendants of Noah and, originally, Adam.

The confusion of the languages led people to scatter across the globe. As people settled in new areas, the traits they carried with them became concentrated in those populations. Traits like dark skin were beneficial in the tropics while other traits benefited populations in northern climates, and distinct people groups, not races, developed.

Other contexts include:

Genetics—the study of human DNA has shown that there is little difference in the genetic makeup of the so-called "races."

Languages—there are about seventy language groups from which all modern languages have developed.

Archaeology—the presence of common building structures, like pyramids, around the world confirms the biblical account.

Literature—recorded and oral records tell of similar events relating to the Flood and the dispersion at Babel.

CHRIST

God did not leave mankind without a way to be redeemed from its sinful state. The Law was given to Moses to show how far away man is from God's standard of perfection. Rather than the sacrifices, which only covered sins, people needed a Savior to take away their sin. This was accomplished when Jesus Christ came to earth to live a perfect life and, by that obedience, was able to be the sacrifice to satisfy God's wrath for all who believe.

The deity of Christ and the amazing plan that was set forth before the foundation of the earth is the core of Christian doctrine. The earthly life of Jesus was the fulfillment of many prophecies and confirms the truthfulness of the Bible. His miracles and presence in human form demonstrate that God is both intimately concerned with His creation and able to control it in an absolute way.

Other contexts include:

Psychology—popular secular psychology teaches of the inherent goodness of man, but Christ has lived the only perfect life. Mankind needs a Savior to redeem it from its unrighteousness.

Biology—Christ's virgin birth demonstrates God's sovereignty over nature.

Physics—turning the water into wine and the feeding of the five thousand demonstrate Christ's deity and His sovereignty over nature.

History—time is marked (in the western world) based on the birth of Christ despite current efforts to change the meaning.

Art—much art is based on the life of Christ and many of the masters are known for these depictions, whether on canvas or in music.

CROSS

Because God is perfectly just and holy, He must punish sin. The sinless life of Jesus Christ was offered as a substitutionary sacrifice for all of those who will repent and put their faith in the Savior. After His death on the Cross, He defeated death by rising on the third day and is now seated at the right hand of God.

The events surrounding the crucifixion and resurrection have a most significant place in the life of Christians. Though there is no way to scientifically prove the resurrection, there is likewise no way to prove the stories of evolutionary history. These are matters of faith founded in the truth of God's Word and His character. The eyewitness testimony of over 500 people and the written Word of God provide the basis for our belief.

Other contexts include:

Biology—the biological details of the crucifixion can be studied alongside the anatomy of the human body.

History—the use of crucifixion as a method of punishment was short-lived in historical terms and not known at the time it was prophesied.

Art—the crucifixion and resurrection have inspired many wonderful works of art.

CONSUMMATION

God, in His great mercy, has promised that He will restore the earth to its original state—a world without death, suffering, war, and disease. The corruption introduced by Adam's sin will be removed.

Those who have repented and put their trust in the completed work of Christ on the Cross will experience life in this new heaven and earth. We will be able to enjoy and worship God forever in a perfect place.

This future event is a little more difficult to connect with academic subjects. However, the hope of a life in God's presence and in the absence of sin can be inserted in discussions of human conflict, disease, suffering, and sin in general.

Other contexts include:

History—in discussions of war or human conflict the coming age offers hope.

Biology—the violent struggle for life seen in the predator-prey relationships will no longer taint the earth.

Medicine—while we struggle to find cures for diseases and alleviate the suffering of those enduring the effects of the Curse, we ultimately place our hope in the healing that will come in the eternal state.

The preceding examples are given to provide ideas for integrating the Seven C's of History into a broad range of curriculum activities. We would recommend that you give your students, and yourself, a better understanding of the Seven C's framework by using AiG's Seven C's of History curriculum. The curriculum provides seven lessons that will establish a solid understanding of the true history, and future, of the universe. Full lesson plans, activities, and student resources are provided in the curriculum set.

We also offer bookmarks displaying the Seven C's and a wall chart. These can be used as visual cues for the students to help them recall the information and integrate new learning into its proper place in a biblical worldview.

Even if you use other curricula, you can still incorporate the Seven C's teaching into those. Using this approach will help students make firm connections between biblical events and every aspect of the world around them, and they will begin to develop a truly biblical worldview and not just add pieces of the Bible to what they learn in "the real world."

OUR UNIVERSE

SPACE MODELS & TOOLS

LESSON 1

INTRODUCTION TO ASTRONOMY

STUDY OF SPACE

SUPPLY LIST

Bible   Copy of "God's Purpose for the Universe" worksheet

Supplies for Challenge: Copy of "Knowledge of the Stars" worksheet

BEGINNERS

- What is astronomy? **The study of the things in space.**

GOD'S PURPOSE FOR THE UNIVERSE WORKSHEET

1. I was designed to rule the day: **Sun/greater light**.

2. I was designed to rule the night: **Moon/lesser light**.

3. We are times that are to be marked by the movement of the sun, moon, and stars: **Seasons, days, and years.**

4. Besides marking times, I am another reason why the sun, moon, and stars were made: **To give light and to show signs.**

5. We were made by God's hands and this is what will eventually happen to us: **Heavens and earth will perish and wear out**.

6. This is higher than me (the earth): **The heavens.**

7. I am what you will see in the heavens in the last days: **Wonders, sun to darkness, moon to blood.**

8. I (the sun), stood still for this long, until Joshua and the Israelites defeated their enemies: **About a full day.**

WHAT DID WE LEARN?

- What is astronomy? **The study of the stars, planets, moons, and other items in space.**

- Why should we want to study astronomy? **To learn more about God's creation and see His glory.**

TAKING IT FURTHER

- What is one thing you really want to learn during this study? **Answers will vary.**

- Write your question or questions on a piece of paper and save it to make sure you find the answers by the end of the book. **Encourage the student to do this and keep it in an accessible place.**

CHALLENGE: KNOWLEDGE OF THE STARS WORKSHEET

1. What is the nearest star to the earth? **Sun.**

2. What are the main elements in stars? **Hydrogen and helium.**

3. What is the name of the galaxy that we live in? **Milky Way.**

4. What is special about Polaris, the North Star? **It does not appear to move through the sky like the other stars.**

5. What unit of distance is used to measure items in space? **Light year, parsec, or astronomical unit.**

6. What name describes when one celestial body blocks the light from another? **Eclipse.**

7. What force holds the planets in their places? **Gravity.**

8. Name three items found in space besides stars, moons, and planets. **Comets, asteroids, meteors, plutoids, space junk, satellites, space station.**

9. Name two scientists important to our understanding of astronomy. **Newton, Galileo, Copernicus, Kepler, Hubble.**

10. How long does it take for light to travel from the sun to the earth? **About 8 minutes.**

LESSON 2

SPACE MODELS

WHAT'S REALLY OUT THERE?

SUPPLY LIST

Book   Piece of paper   Ping-pong ball   Golf ball

BEGINNERS

- Does the sun move around the earth or does the earth move around the sun? **The earth moves around the sun.**

- What force keeps all the planets, moons, and stars in their places? **Gravity.**

WHAT DID WE LEARN?

- What are the two major models that have been used to describe the arrangement of the universe? **Geocentric/Ptolemaic—earth centered, and Heliocentric/Copernican—sun centered.**

- What was the main idea of the Geocentric Model? **The earth was the center of the universe and everything revolved around it.**

- What is the main idea of the Heliocentric Model? **The sun is the center of the solar system and the earth and other planets revolve around it.**

- What force holds all of the planets in orbit around the sun? **Gravity.**

TAKING IT FURTHER

- Which exerts the most gravitational pull, the earth or the sun? **The sun because it is much more massive than the earth.**

- If the sun has a stronger gravitational pull, then why aren't objects pulled off of the earth toward the sun? **The strength of the gravitational pull decreases with distance. The pull of the earth is stronger on us because we are so much closer to the center of the earth than we are to the sun. If an object moves far enough away from the earth, the earth's gravity no longer has much effect on it. And if that object moves close enough to the sun, it will be pulled into the sun by the sun's gravity.**

LESSON 3

THE EARTH'S MOVEMENT

ROTATING AND REVOLVING

SUPPLY LIST

Flashlight   Basketball or volleyball   Masking tape
Supplies for Challenge: Copy of "Clock" pattern   Tripod   Thread   Needle
Modeling clay   Turntable, swivel chair or stool, Lazy Susan, etc.

BEGINNERS

- In what two ways is the earth moving? **Rotating on its axis and orbiting or revolving around the sun.**

- Why do we experience seasons like summer and winter? **The earth is tilted with respect to the sun. When your part of the earth is tilted toward the sun it is summer, and when it is tilted away from the sun it is winter.**

WHAT DID WE LEARN?

- What are the two different types of motion that the earth experiences? **Rotation on its axis and revolution around the sun.**

- What observations can we make that are the result of the rotation of the earth on its axis? **Day and night, the stars rotating in the sky, the bulging of the earth, diagonal air flow.**

- What observations can we make that are the result of the revolution of the earth around the sun? **Changing of the seasons, parallax of stars, more meteors observed after midnight.**

- What is a solstice? **The first day of summer or the first day of winter, when the earth is in the place in its orbit where the sun is hitting directly on either the Tropic of Cancer or the Tropic of Capricorn.**

- What is an equinox? **The first day of spring or the first day of autumn, when the earth is halfway between the solstices.**

TAKING IT FURTHER

- What are the advantages of the earth being tilted on its axis as it revolves around the sun? **This gives us seasons. Without this tilt, the temperatures would be relatively stable year round. This would result in less of the earth being able to grow crops. Only the warm areas near the equator would have warm enough weather to grow food.**

- One argument against Copernicus's theory was that if the earth were moving, flying birds would be left behind. Why don't the birds get left behind as the earth moves through space? **The atmosphere in which the birds are flying moves with the earth because of gravity.**

CHALLENGE: FOUCAULT PENDULUM

- What forces are affecting the pendulum? **Gravity is pulling down on the weight at the end of the pendulum, and air is resisting the movement of the pendulum.**

- Why does the pendulum eventually stop moving? **Because of the air resistance.**

- How does a Foucault pendulum keep moving for hours or days at a time without stopping? **They are often designed with an iron ring near the top where the pendulum is attached to the building. Also, there are electromagnets placed around the ring. As the pendulum swings through a certain part of its arc the magnet turns on, attracting the ring. Then the magnet turns off to allow the pendulum to swing freely. This magnet system compensates for the air resistance that the pendulum experiences, so it does not slow down.**

LESSON 4

TOOLS FOR STUDYING SPACE

DO I NEED MORE THAN MY EYES?

SUPPLY LIST

Mirror   Magnifying glass   Flashlight   Optional: Access to a telescope

Supplies for Challenge: Paper   Marker   Car

BEGINNERS

- What is a telescope and what is it used for? **An instrument with lenses and mirrors that makes something look bigger. It is used to view distant objects like stars, planets, and other things in space.**

WHAT DID WE LEARN?

- What are the three main types of telescopes? **Refracting—using only lenses, Reflecting—using lenses and mirrors, Radio—collecting radio waves.**
- What was one disadvantage of the early refracting telescope? **The refracting lens bent the light causing false colors to appear around the edges of the image.**
- How did Newton avoid this problem? **He used mirrors instead of a lens to collect the light.**

TAKING IT FURTHER

- Why do you think scientists wanted to put a telescope in space? **It would give better images without the interference of the earth's atmosphere. It would also not be affected by the movement of the earth and it would not be limited to one position on the earth.**
- What kinds of things can we learn from using optical telescopes? **What a star looks like, its color, brilliance, etc. Astronomers have observed that occasionally what appears to be only one star might actually be two stars.**
- What kinds of things can we learn from radio telescopes? **The radio wave activity of a star or other object in space can be detected. Different substances emit different wavelengths of radio waves so the composition of a star can be determined. Also, using radio waves as radar allows us to get an idea of the density of planets.**

QUIZ 1

SPACE MODELS & TOOLS

LESSONS 1–4

Short answer:

1. What are the two ways the earth moves in space? **Rotates on axis, revolves around sun.**
2. Why does the earth experience seasons? **Its axis is tilted with respect to the sun.**
3. Why are seasons an indication of God's provision for man? **The seasons allow more of the earth to be cultivated for food.**
4. What is the main idea of the Geocentric Model? **The earth is the center of our solar system/universe.**
5. What is the main idea of the Heliocentric Model? **The sun is the center of our solar system.**

Mark each statement either True or False.

6. _F_ Scientists can prove where the earth came from.

7. _F_ Scientists have proven the Big Bang is true.

8. _T_ The Bible can tell us some things about astronomy.

9. _F_ The Bible can tell us everything about astronomy.

10. _T_ Gravity is the force that holds all planets in orbit.

11. _F_ Galileo invented the first telescope.

12. _T_ Heavier objects exert more gravity than lighter objects.

13. _T_ Closer objects exert more gravity than ones farther away.

14. _F_ The sun exerts more gravity on us than the earth does.

15. _T_ The Bible says that God's power can be seen in His creation.

16. _T_ Newton's reflecting telescope reduced chromatic aberration.

CHALLENGE QUESTIONS

Short answer:

17. List at least one contribution that each of the following men made to the study of astronomy:

    Nicolaus Copernicus: **Developed the Heliocentric Model of the solar system**.

    Galileo: **First to use a telescope to study the heavens, discovered moons around Jupiter and rings around Saturn, supported Heliocentric Model.**

    Sir Isaac Newton: **Defined the laws of gravitation, developed a reflecting telescope to reduce chromatic aberration.**

18. What invention did you study that demonstrates the rotation of the earth? **Foucault pendulum.**

19. Why do scientists look for ways to make telescopes larger? **Larger telescopes gather more light and give brighter, clearer images.**

20. Explain briefly how the mirror of the Keck telescope is made? **The Keck telescope mirror consists of many hexagon shaped mirrors that fit together to form a very large mirror.**

UNIT 2
OUTER SPACE

OVERVIEW OF THE UNIVERSE

HOW BIG IS IT?

SUPPLY LIST

Star chart   Clear night sky

BEGINNERS

- What objects make up our solar system? **The sun and all the things that orbit it.**

- What is a constellation? **A collection of stars that make a particular picture.**

- Why did sailors need to be able to recognize stars? **So they could locate them in the night sky and use them for navigation.**

WHAT DID WE LEARN?

- What is our solar system? **The group of heavenly bodies that includes our sun and the planets that revolve around it.**

- Our solar system is part of which galaxy? **The Milky Way galaxy.**

- How big is the universe? **No one knows for sure. Some people believe that is has no end.**

TAKING IT FURTHER

- Why do you think our galaxy is called the Milky Way? **Because on clear nights the stars in the galaxy make a white milky band across the sky.**

- Why do you need star charts that are different for different times of the year? **Because as the earth travels around the sun, it is in a slightly different position with respect to the stars each day.**

- Why do you need star charts that are different for different times of the night? **Because as the earth rotates on its axis, a particular spot on the earth moves with respect to the stars.**

CHALLENGE: LOCATING STARS

- Explain how a star map is similar to a map of the globe. **They both have an equator and prime longitude line. They both allow you to locate areas using the equivalent of latitude and longitude.**

- What units are used to measure declination and ascension? **Declination—degrees north or south, ascension—hours and minutes.**

- How does an astronomer define a constellation differently than most people? **To an astronomer, a constellation is an area in the sky; to most people, a constellation is a collection of stars that forms a picture of sorts.**

LESSON 6

STARS

TWINKLE, TWINKLE LITTLE STAR

SUPPLY LIST

Copy of "Starlight" worksheet   Ruler and a yardstick
2 flashlights (one brighter than the other or with different sizes of lenses)
Supplies for Challenge: Calculator

BEGINNERS

- Why might some stars look different from other stars? **They are different colors; some are farther away; they are made from different materials;some are brighter.**

STARLIGHT WORKSHEET

- What happened to the light beam as the flashlight was moved farther from the wall? **The beam got wider but was not as intense; the closer one would appear brighter.**

- How would two identical stars appear to someone on earth if one was much farther away? **The one farther away would appear smaller and dimmer than the closer one.**

- Why could two stars with the same apparent brightness be different distances from the earth? **Because the way the stars appear to us is determined by the brightness of the star and the distance to the star; if one star was much brighter than the other but also farther away, the same amount of light could be hitting the earth from both stars. This would make them appear the same to us.**

WHAT DID WE LEARN?

- What is the unit of distance used to measure how far away something is in space? **Light-year.**

- How far is a light-year? **The distance light travels in one year—about 6 trillion miles.**

- What does the color of a star tell us about that star? **Its approximate surface temperature; blue stars are much hotter than yellow or red stars.**

TAKING IT FURTHER

- What causes stars to appear to move in the sky? **Most apparent motion is caused by the movement of the earth.**

- How can we determine if a star's absolute distance from the earth is actually changing over time? **We must measure its light over a long period of time and see if it is changing.**

- Why is brightness not a good indicator of the distance of a star from the earth? **Brightness is determined by the amount of light emitted and how far the star is from the earth. Brighter stars may be farther away but emitting more light, or they may be closer and emitting less light. You need to know how much light is being emitted, as well as the brightness, to determine the distance of the star from earth.**

LESSON 7
HEAVENLY BODIES
MORE THAN JUST STARS

SUPPLY LIST

Flashlight   Pencil

BEGINNERS

- What is a galaxy? **A large group of stars that rotates together.**
- What is the name of our galaxy? **The Milky Way.**

WHAT DID WE LEARN?

- What is a cluster of stars? **A group of stars that appear to move together.**
- What is a galaxy? **A group of millions (or billions) of stars that rotates around a central point.**
- Explain the difference between a nova, a supernova, and a neutron star. **A nova is a star that is exploding and then returns to normal. A supernova is a star that experiences such a huge explosion that it may be destroyed. A neutron star is believed to be what is left of a supernova. It is extremely small and dense and emits radio waves.**

TAKING IT FURTHER

- How can a star appear to become brighter and dimmer on a regular basis? **If two stars rotate around each other, they can line up so that they appear as one bright star. Later, one star can block the light of the other making it appear dimmer. Also, some stars expand and contract on a regular basis causing them to appear brighter and dimmer—these are called Cepheid variable stars.**
- Why does starlight from millions of light-years away not prove that the earth is old? **There are several ideas using general relativity that explain how time may have passed more slowly on earth while billions of years were passing on the stars in the expanding universe.**

LESSON 8
ASTEROIDS
MINOR PLANETS

SUPPLY LIST

Paper and pencil
Supplies for Challenge: Research materials for the Trojan War

BEGINNERS

- What is an asteroid? **A large piece of rock orbiting the sun.**
- Where is the asteroid belt located? **Between the orbits of Mars and Jupiter.**

WHAT DID WE LEARN?

- What is an asteroid? **A relatively small rock in a regular orbit around the sun.**
- Where are most asteroids in our solar system located? **In the asteroid belt between the orbits of Mars and Jupiter.**
- What is another name for asteroids? **Minor planets.**

TAKING IT FURTHER

- What is the chance that an asteroid will hit the earth? **Relatively small. As Christians we must trust God that all things, including asteroids, are in His control.**

CHALLENGE: TROJAN ASTEROIDS

- **Some of the names of the Trojan asteroids include: Achilles, Hektor, Nestor, Agamemnon, Odysseus, Ajax, Diomedes, Antilochus, and Menelaus.**

LESSON 9

COMETS

LOOK AT THAT TAIL!

SUPPLY LIST

Small Styrofoam ball   Tagboard/poster board   Glue   Glitter

BEGINNERS

- What is a comet? **A ball of ice and dust that orbits the sun.**
- What are the two parts of a comet? **The head and the tail.**

WHAT DID WE LEARN?

- What is a comet? **A frozen core of rock and dust that orbits the sun in a regular orbit.**
- Who was the first person to accurately predict the orbit of comets? **Edmond Halley.**
- What are the two main parts of a comet? **Head, tail.**

TAKING IT FURTHER

- Why does a comet's tail always point away from the sun? **The solar winds that cause the tail are always moving away from the sun.**
- Why doesn't a comet have a tail when it is far from the sun? **There are no solar winds to push it, and it does not vaporize when it is far from the sun.**
- When will Halley's Comet next appear? **1986 + 75 = 2061.**

CHALLENGE: GOD CREATED COMETS

1. **Comets become smaller every time they pass the sun. Thus they are wearing out just as the earth and the rest of the universe is wearing out.**
2. **Comets make regular paths around the sun, thus they can be used for telling seasons, days, and years.**

3. **Many cultures, especially ancient cultures, viewed unusual activity in the heavens as bad omens, so the appearance of a comet would have been considered a bad omen. But God says not to be dismayed by them. Because they have regular orbits, their appearances can be predicted and there is nothing to fear.**

4. **There is no evidence for a comet nursery; comets were created in the beginning by God.**

LESSON 10
METEORS
SHOOTING STARS

SUPPLY LIST

Pie pan   Salt   Flour   Marble   Toys   Golf ball

BEGINNERS

- What is a meteor? **A rock that is pulled into the earth's atmosphere and burns up.**

- Where do many meteors come from? **Broken up comets.**

WHAT DID WE LEARN?

- What is the difference between a meteoroid, meteor, and meteorite? **Meteoroids are small pieces of rock and other debris floating in space—usually orbiting the sun. Meteors are meteoroids that get close enough to the earth to be pulled in by the earth's gravity. Meteorites are meteors that reach the surface of the earth.**

- When is the best time to watch for meteors? **After midnight on any evening and especially around August 12 and November 17.**

TAKING IT FURTHER

- Space dust (extremely small meteorites) is constantly falling on the earth. If this has been going on for billions of years, what would you expect to find on the earth and in the oceans? **You would expect to find many meteorites in the fossil layers. You would also expect to find many feet of space dust accumulating in the oceans.**

- Have we discovered these things? **No. There have been very few confirmed meteorites found in the fossil layers, and a very small amount of space dust found in the oceans. Both of these facts indicate that the earth is relatively young.**

QUIZ 2
OUTER SPACE
LESSONS 5–10

Match the term with its definition.

1. _C_ Millions of stars rotating around a center

2. _L_ Name of our galaxy

3. _F_ Collection of planets orbiting the sun

4. _I_ A group of stars that form a picture

5. _B_ Star that doesn't move with respect to the earth's rotation

6. _A_ Unit of measurement for distances in space

7. _E_ An exploding star

8. _H_ Cloud of gas and dust in space

9. _K_ Scientific study of the universe/space

10. _M_ Superstitious belief that stars control the future

11. _D_ Gap between Mars and Jupiter

12. _G_ Balls of ice that orbit the sun

13. _J_ Piece of space debris that reaches the earth's surface

14. _O_ Piece of space debris that burns up in the atmosphere

15. _N_ What you can tell from a star's color

Short answer:

16. If a star has a blue color, is it hotter or cooler than our sun? **Hotter.**

17. What two things do we need to know to determine how far away a star is? **Brightness and amount of light emitted.**

18. Why do stars appear to move through the night sky? **Primarily earth's rotation (earth's revolution causes the starts to be in a different location from one night to the next).**

CHALLENGE QUESTIONS

Short answer:

19. Where do many evolutionists believe new stars are formed? Why is this unlikely? **In nebulae. Gas is expanding not contracting in nebulae.**

20. What names are given on a star map for the lines that are projected from the equator and the prime meridian? **Celestial equator and prime hour circle.**

21. What is the most common evolutionary explanation for the origins of the universe? **Big bang theory.**

22. Give one possible explanation for the ability to see distant starlight in a young world. **Earth is at the center of the universe and more time passed at the outer regions while the universe was expanding during creation than passed on earth. Another possible answer is that the speed of light was faster in the past.**

23. What is a group of asteroids traveling in the same path called? **A family.**

24. Name three asteroids in the Trojan Family. **Achilles, Hektor, Nestor, Agamemnon, Odysseus, Ajax, Diomedes, Antilochus, and Menelaus.**

25. Why does the existence of comets indicate that the universe is young? **Comets only exist for a few thousand years and we do not have any evidence that new comets are being formed.**

26. What is the most likely explanation for the extinction of dinosaurs? **Failure to adapt to changed climate after the Flood.**

UNIT 3
SUN & MOON

LESSON 11

OVERVIEW OF OUR SOLAR SYSTEM

REVOLVING AROUND THE SUN

SUPPLY LIST

A willingness to sing
Supplies for Challenge: Cardboard   String   2 thumb tacks   Paper

BEGINNERS

- How many planets are in our solar system? **8 (Pluto is no longer considered a planet).**
- What are the names of the small planets? **Mercury, Venus, Earth, Mars.**
- What are the names of the large planets? **Jupiter, Saturn, Uranus, Neptune.**

WHAT DID WE LEARN?

- Name the eight planets in our solar system. **Mercury, Venus, Earth, Mars, Jupiter, Saturn, Uranus, and Neptune—Pluto is no longer considered a planet, but a plutoid.**
- Name two of the plutoids. **Ceres, Pluto, and Eris were mentioned in this lesson.**
- Which planets can support life? **Only earth.**

TAKING IT FURTHER

- What are the major differences between the inner and outer planets? **Inner planets are closer to the sun, smaller, and are terrestrial (solid rock). Outer planets are larger and made from gas.**
- Why are the gas planets called Jovian planets? **Jovian means Jupiter-like. Jupiter is a gas giant. The other planets that are also comprised of gas, like Jupiter, are thus called Jovian.**

LESSON 12

OUR SUN

THE CENTER OF OUR SOLAR SYSTEM

SUPPLY LIST

Pie pan   Small mirror   Prism (optional)

Supplies for Challenge: Copy of "Sun Measurement" worksheet 2 index cards Needle
Meter stick Ruler Tape Calculator

BEGINNERS

- What is the sun? **A star in the center of our solar system.**
- What two things does the sun provide for the earth? **Heat and light.**
- How long does it take for the earth to go around the sun one time? **One year.**

WHAT DID WE LEARN?

- What are the main elements found in the sun? **95% of the sun is hydrogen and helium.**
- What colors are found in sunlight? **All colors from violet to red.**

TAKING IT FURTHER

- Why is the sun so important to us? **Its gravity holds everything in our solar system in place; it provides heat, light, and energy for life.**
- How does energy get from the sun to the earth? **It travels in waves—light, heat, radio, and x-rays.**

CHALLENGE: MEASUREMENT WORKSHEET

- What could account for the differences in your calculated value versus the known value? **The circle is small, so exact measurements are difficult to make. This causes error so your answer will differ from the expected value.**
- How does the diameter of the sun compare with the diameter of the earth? **The diameter of the earth is approximately 7,927 miles. The diameter of the sun is about 109 times bigger.**

LESSON 13 STRUCTURE OF THE SUN

WHAT IS IT LIKE ON THE INSIDE?

SUPPLY LIST

Sidewalk chalk Note: It is most effective if you start this project in the morning.

BEGINNERS

- What are the two things the sun is made from? **Hydrogen and helium.**
- Why should you never look directly at the sun? **It can damage your eyes.**
- What are cooler areas of the sun called? **Sunspots.**

WHAT DID WE LEARN?

- What are the two parts of the sun's atmosphere? **The chromosphere and the corona.**
- What is a sunspot? **An area on the sun's surface that is cooler than surrounding areas.**
- Are sunspots stationary? **No, they tend to move from east to west across the surface of the sun.**
- What do scientists believe are the three parts of the sun's interior? **The core, radiative zone, and convective zone.**

TAKING IT FURTHER

- What is the hottest part of the sun? **The core, which is believed to be nearly 25 million degrees Fahrenheit.**

- What causes the aurora borealis or northern lights? **Particles emitted by a solar flare light up when they reach the earth's ionosphere.**

- When do you think scientists study the sun's corona? **The best time is during a solar eclipse. Scientists can see and study the corona while the rest of the sun is hidden by the moon.**

LESSON 14

SOLAR ECLIPSE
WHERE DID IT GO?

SUPPLY LIST

Flashlight   Tennis ball   Basketball or volleyball

Supplies for Challenge: Research materials on future lunar and solar eclipses

BEGINNERS

- What is a solar eclipse? **When the moon comes between the sun and the earth and blocks the sun's light from reaching the earth.**

- Does an eclipse block the light from the whole earth at once? **No, only a small area would be affected by an eclipse.**

- How often does an eclipse happen? **1 to 3 times a year.**

WHAT DID WE LEARN?

- What is an eclipse? **When one heavenly body blocks the light from another heavenly body.**

- What is the difference between a partial and a total eclipse? **A partial eclipse only covers part of the sun's disk, while a total eclipse covers it completely.**

- How often do solar eclipses occur? **1 to 3 times each year.**

TAKING IT FURTHER

- Why do you think plants and animals start preparing for nightfall during an eclipse? **Their instincts tell them that the sun is going down.**

- Why can a total eclipse only be seen in a small area on the earth? **The shadow of the moon is only about 150 miles across.**

- How can the moon block out the entire sun when the sun is 400 times bigger than the moon? **The moon is 400 times closer to the earth than the sun is, so from the earth they appear to be about the same size.**

LESSON 15

SOLAR ENERGY

CAN IT MEET OUR ENERGY NEEDS?

SUPPLY LIST

Copy of "Solar Energy" worksheet   Black, white, and green construction paper
2 clear glasses   Thermometer   Ice   Scissors and tape
Supplies for Challenge: Hardback books   Flashlight   Clipboard   Paper   Pencil

BEGINNERS

• What is solar energy? **Energy we get from the sun.**

• What are two ways that people use solar energy? **To heat water and to make electricity.**

SOLAR ENERGY WORKSHEET

• What color would you use to paint a solar collector? **Dark colors absorb more heat than light colors and dull surfaces absorb more heat than shiny ones. So solar collectors are painted with a dull black paint.**

WHAT DID WE LEARN?

• What is solar energy? **Energy we get from the sun.**

• What are the two ways that solar energy is used today? **To heat water and to generate electricity.**

TAKING IT FURTHER

• Why is solar energy a good alternative to fossil fuels? **It is clean, readily available, and virtually unlimited.**

• Why are the insides of solar collectors painted black? **Black absorbs the heat from the sun so black solar collectors are more efficient than other colors would be.**

• What are some of the advantages of using solar cells in outer space? **Other fuel sources would be too heavy to launch into space, but solar panels are very light. The sun shines all the time in space and there is no atmosphere to block the sun's energy.**

CHALLENGE: SOLAR ENERGY

• Is the new pattern bigger or smaller than the first pattern? **It should be bigger. The same amount of light is hitting the paper in both instances, but when the paper is at an angle, the light is more spread out, or dispersed.**

• Based on what you just learned, where would be the best location for a solar energy power plant? **The light hits the earth most directly at the equator, so a solar power plant would work best near the equator in an area that gets relatively few clouds.**

LESSON 16

OUR MOON

IS IT MADE OF GREEN CHEESE?

SUPPLY LIST

Reflector (like one from a bicycle)   Flashlight
Supplies for Challenge: Binoculars or telescope (if available)

BEGINNERS

- Does the moon make its own light? **No.**
- Where does the moon's light come from? **The moon's light is light that is reflected from the sun.**
- How is the moon's surface different from the earth's surface? **It has no air and no plants or animals. It has many craters.**

WHAT DID WE LEARN?

- Why does the moon shine? **It reflects the light from the sun**.
- What causes the dark spots on the surface of the moon? **They are plains that are covered with hardened basalt.**

TAKING IT FURTHER

- Why does the size of our moon show God's provision for man? **It is much larger than most moons. This allows it to reflect a significant amount of light, lighting up the night.**
- Why is gravity much less on the moon than on the earth? **The moon is much less massive than the earth, and gravity is a function of mass.**
- Why doesn't the surface of the earth have as many craters as the surface of the moon? **Most meteors burn up in our atmosphere before they reach the earth's surface, but the moon does not have an atmosphere to protect it.**

LESSON 17

MOTION & PHASES OF THE MOON

THERE'S A FULL MOON TONIGHT

SUPPLY LIST

Copy of "Identifying Phases of the Moon" worksheet
Supplies for Challenge: Copy of "Observing the Phases of the Moon" worksheet

BEGINNERS

- What two ways does the moon move? **Rotates on its axis, revolves around earth.**
- What is a new moon? **When the moon does not reflect any sunlight.**

Identifying Phases of the Moon worksheet

1. **New moon**
2. **Waxing crescent**
3. **First quarter**
4. **Waxing gibbous**
5. **Full moon**
6. **Waning gibbous**
7. **Last quarter**
8. **Waning crescent**

What did we learn?

- What causes the phases of the moon? **The orbit of the moon around the earth causes it to be in a different position with respect to the sun each day.**

- Why does the same side of the moon always face the earth? **The moon rotates on its axis at the same rate that is revolves around the earth.**

- What causes a lunar eclipse? **The earth passes directly between the moon and the sun, blocking the light of the sun from the moon.**

- From the perspective of space, how long does it take for the moon to complete its cycle around the earth? **27.3 days, or about a month.**

Taking it further

- Why doesn't a lunar eclipse occur every month? **The moon's orbit is tilted 5 degrees from the earth's orbit so the sun, earth, and moon don't line up perfectly very often.**

- What is the difference between a waxing crescent and a waning crescent? **The waxing crescent is lit up on the right side of the moon from the earth's perspective, and is getting larger; the waning crescent is lit up on the left side of the moon, and is getting smaller.**

Challenge: Observing the Moon

- When is the light side of the moon the same as the near side of the moon? **Full moon.**

- When is the dark side of the moon the same as the near side of the moon? **New moon.**

LESSON 18
Origin of the Moon
Where did it come from?

Supply list

2 tops (spinning toys)   Masking tape
Supplies for Challenge: Bible

Beginners

- Where did the earth come from? **God created it.**
- Where did the moon come from? **God created it, too.**
- On which day of creation did God create the moon? **Day 4.**

What did we learn?

- What are four secular theories for the origin of the moon? **Capture Theory, Fission Theory, Accretion, and Impact Theory.**

- Which of these theories is most likely to be true? **None. They all have significant problems.**

- What does the Bible say about the origin of the moon? **It says that God created the moon on Day 4 to light up the night.**

Taking it further

- What are the main difficulties with the Capture Theory? **Scientists cannot explain what would cause the moon to leave its original orbit. The probability that the moon would approach the earth at exactly the right angle and speed to result in the moon orbiting the earth is extremely small.**

- Why do you think scientists come up with unworkable ideas for the moon's origin? **Scientists try to find answers to important questions. They come up with ideas for possible solutions. These are called hypotheses. They then test their hypotheses to see if they are true or not. Sometimes a hypothesis is wrong and should be cast aside. Generally, there are two problems with hypotheses concerning origins: 1. We cannot adequately test them because we cannot recreate the conditions under which the event took place; and 2. Many scientists are unwilling to consider the option that God exists, much less that He created things; therefore, many scientists still cling to unworkable ideas rather than admit that something outside of natural causes exists.**

Challenge: Origin of the Moon

- **Genesis 1:14–19 - God spoke the moon into existence on the fourth day of creation. Ps. 8:3–4 - The moon is the work of God's fingers; He set it in place. Ps. 33:6 - The heavens were made by God's word. Ps. 74:16 - God established the moon. Ps. 136:3–9 - God made the moon by His understanding (or wisdom). Jer. 31:35 - The Lord decreed the moon to shine.**

- **These verses clearly show that God created the moon out of nothing by speaking it into existence. They adequately explain the origin of the moon. The naturalistic explanations all have significant problems that cannot be explained by naturalistic means.**

QUIZ 3

Sun & Moon

Lessons 11–18

List the planets in our solar system in order from the closest to the sun outward. **Mercury, Venus, Earth, Mars, Jupiter, Saturn, Uranus, Neptune.**

Mark each statement as either True or False.

1. _F_ A lunar eclipse occurs when the moon blocks the light from the sun.
2. _T_ The energy from the sun is generated by a process similar to a hydrogen bomb.
3. _F_ Scientists can directly view the interior of the sun.
4. _F_ The aurora borealis is a result of sunspots.
5. _F_ A total solar eclipse causes the whole earth to become dark.
6. _T_ Animals may act like night is falling during a solar eclipse.
7. _T_ It is very dangerous to look at the sun even during a total eclipse.
8. _F_ Solar collectors work best if they are painted glossy white.
9. _T_ Solar cells convert the sun's rays into electricity.
10. _T_ The same side of the moon always faces the earth.
11. _F_ Maria are areas on the moon filled with water.

12. _**T**_ The moon does not generate its own light.

Fill in the blank with the correct term.

13. The moon is called a _**full**_ moon when it is on the opposite side of the earth from the sun.

14. The moon is called a _**new**_ moon when it is on the same side of the earth as the sun.

15. The main elements found in the sun are _**hydrogen and helium**_.

CHALLENGE QUESTIONS

Match the term with its definition.

16. _**B**_ Squashed circle
17. _**C**_ Place in orbit closest to the sun
18. _**G**_ Place in orbit farthest from the sun
19. _**J**_ Center of a sunspot
20. _**D**_ Outer edge of a sunspot
21. _**E**_ Not concentrated
22. _**F**_ Plain filled with hardened basalt
23. _**K**_ Depression made by a meteorite
24. _**I**_ Valley on the moon
25. _**A**_ Side of the moon facing the earth
26. _**L**_ Side of the moon facing away from the earth
27. _**H**_ The side of the moon facing away from the sun

PLANETS

LESSON 19

MERCURY

CLOSEST PLANET TO THE SUN

SUPPLY LIST

Towel   Hair dryer   Ice

Supplies for Challenge: 2 index cards   Flashlight   2 clear plastic cups   Magnifying glass

BEGINNERS

- Name three things you learned about Mercury? **It is closest to the sun; it is the second smallest planet; it has very little atmosphere; it gets very hot and very cold.**

WHAT DID WE LEARN?

- How does Mercury's revolution around the sun and rotation on its axis compare to that of the earth? **Mercury travels quickly around the sun, but turns slowly on its axis compared to earth.**
- What is the surface of Mercury like? **Very hot or very cold, solid with lots of craters.**

TAKING IT FURTHER

- How does a lack of atmosphere affect the conditions on Mercury? **It causes extreme temperature swings and allows meteorites to strike the surface.**

LESSON 20

VENUS

THE SECOND PLANET

SUPPLY LIST

Copy of "Greenhouse Effect" worksheet   Shoebox   Plastic wrap   Aluminum foil   Tape Thermometer

Supplies for Challenge: Shoebox   Modeling clay   Graph paper   Ruler   String   Washer

BEGINNERS

- What is the name of the second planet from the sun? **Venus.**
- Why couldn't you live on Venus? **It has a poisonous atmosphere and it is too hot.**

- Why can we see Venus in the night sky? **Its clouds reflect sunlight making it very bright.**

GREENHOUSE EFFECT WORKSHEET

- What did you observe about the temperature in the box when it was covered with plastic wrap? **The temperature goes up inside the box.**
- Why did the temperature do this? **The plastic wrap traps some of the sun's rays.**
- What do you think the temperature would be inside the box if you left it in the sun for several hours? **The temperature will continue to rise for some time and then level off**.

WHAT DID WE LEARN?

- Where is Venus's orbit with respect to the sun and the other planets? **It is second from the sun.**
- What makes Venus so bright in the sky? **Its atmosphere reflects the light of the sun.**
- What is a nickname for Venus? **The Morning Star or the Evening Star.**
- How many moons does Venus have? **None.**

TAKING IT FURTHER

- Even though Venus has an atmosphere, why can't life exist there? **The atmosphere is poisonous to people, plants, and animals. Also, it makes the planet too hot. The thick atmosphere also exerts too much pressure and would crush any living creatures.**
- Why doesn't the earth's atmosphere keep our planet too hot? **It is not nearly as thick as the atmosphere on Venus and it is composed of different gases. There is some concern about the greenhouse effect increasing on the earth because of increased carbon dioxide in the air. Some scientists feel that this is a real threat, while others feel that it is not. Most evidence points to higher carbon dioxide levels in the past, which may have actually been beneficial and not harmful. More study is needed in this area.**

LESSON 21

EARTH

DESIGNED FOR LIFE

SUPPLY LIST

1 orange per child	Markers	Globe of the earth	World map
Supplies for Challenge: 2 clear cups	Water	Milk	Flashlight

BEGINNERS

- What is the third planet from the sun? **Earth.**
- List three ways that earth is just right for life. **Right distance from the sun, lots of water, good atmosphere.**
- How long does it take for the earth to make one trip around the sun? **1 year.**
- How long does it take for the earth to rotate once on its axis? **1 day.**

WHAT DID WE LEARN?

- What are some features of our planet that make it uniquely able to support life? **Just the right distance from the sun, axis is tilted just right to make most of the earth able to grow food, large amount of water, right atmosphere and weather patterns.**
- What name is given to the period of time it takes for the earth's revolution around the sun? **Year.**
- What name is given to the length of the earth's rotation on its axis? **Day.**
- On average, how far is the earth from the sun? **About 93 million miles or 150 million km.**

TAKING IT FURTHER

- What are some possible reasons why large amounts of water are found on earth but not on other planets? **Some planets are too hot and water evaporates away; some planets do not have enough gravity to hold an atmosphere so water also evaporates away; other planets do not have the right elements readily available; but most importantly, God created this planet uniquely for us.**
- Why is it important that earth is a terrestrial planet? **This means earth has a solid surface for us to live on.**

LESSON 22 — MARS

THE RED PLANET

SUPPLY LIST

Empty aquarium or other case   Gloves   Liquid dish soap   Matches   Cup   Candle
Dry ice (Note: Dry ice must be obtained shortly before it is needed and must be handled by an adult with gloves.)
Supplies for Challenge: Research materials on Mars space probes

BEGINNERS

- What is the name of the fourth planet from the sun? **Mars.**
- How big is Mars compared to earth? **About half as big.**
- Why is Mars sometimes called the red planet? **It has rust in its soil giving it a red tint.**

EXPERIMENTING WITH POLAR ICE CAPS

- What was the "smoke" coming off of the dry ice? **Carbon dioxide gas.**
- Why did the candle flame go out? **The carbon dioxide in the cup was heavier than air and pushed the oxygen away from the candle so the flame went out.**
- Why did the water in the cup "boil"? **As the dry ice melted it quickly turned to gas, which bubbled to the surface of the water.**

WHAT DID WE LEARN?

- Why is Mars called a superior planet? **It has an orbit that is larger than the earth's orbit.**
- Why is Mars called the red planet? **Its soil has a red color due to a high amount of iron oxide—rust.**
- How many moons does Mars have? **2—Phobos and Deimos.**

TAKING IT FURTHER

- What causes the dust storms on Mars? **Heat from the sun causes winds that pick up dust**.

- Why doesn't the wind on earth cause giant dust storms like the wind on Mars? **Although heat from the sun does cause wind, most of the earth is covered with water. Also, the land is mostly covered with vegetation that holds down the soil, so giant dust storms are unlikely. Small dust and sand storms do happen on earth.**

- How would your weight on Mars compare to your weight on Mercury? **They would be about the same because the gravity it about the same on both planets.**

LESSON 23

JUPITER

THE GAS GIANT

SUPPLY LIST

2 cereal bowls   Marbles—enough to fill both bowls

Supplies for Challenge: Clear cup   Water   Tea bag   Pencil

BEGINNERS

- What is the name of the fifth planet? **Jupiter.**

- Name three things that are special about Jupiter. **It is made of gas not rock, it is the largest planet, it has a Great Red Spot, it has more than 60 moons.**

WHAT DID WE LEARN?

- What are some major differences between Jupiter and the inner planets? **The inner planets are solid and relatively small. Jupiter is very large and made of gas.**

- What is the Great Red Spot? **It is believed to be a giant wind storm that has lasted hundreds of years.**

TAKING IT FURTHER

- Why does Jupiter bulge more in the middle than earth does? **Jupiter spins faster on its axis than the earth does, causing more outward or centrifugal force.**

- Why can't life exist on Jupiter? **The temperatures are too cold, the surface is not solid, there is no air to breathe.**

- Why are space probes necessary for exploring other planets? **Probes can go where people can't. They can see things up close that we cannot see from earth. For example, Voyager discovered a ring around Jupiter. Also, probes can go into environments that are difficult for humans to enter such as Venus's carbon dioxide and sulfuric acid atmosphere. Probes can do tests in far away places like the soil tests done on Mars by the Spirit and Opportunity rovers.**

LESSON 24

SATURN

SURROUNDED BY BEAUTIFUL RINGS

SUPPLY LIST (none)

BEGINNERS

- What are Saturn's rings made from? **Ice, dust, and rocks.**
- What is the name of Saturn's largest moon? **Titan.**

WHAT DID WE LEARN?

- Who first saw Saturn's rings? **Galileo; however he did not recognize them as rings. Christian Huygens first identified the rings.**
- What are Saturn's rings made of? **Pieces of ice, dust, and rock.**
- What makes Titan unique among moons? **It is the only moon with an atmosphere.**

TAKING IT FURTHER

- Why did astronomers believe that Saturn had only a few rings before the Voyager space probe explored Saturn? **That was all that could be observed from earth using telescopes.**
- Both Titan and earth have a mostly nitrogen atmosphere. What important differences exist between these two worlds that make earth able to support life but Titan unable to? **Titan is too far away from the sun, and thus is too cold to support life. Also, Titan's atmosphere has methane and no oxygen. Earth has just the right amount of oxygen to support life.**

LESSON 25

URANUS

SEVENTH PLANET FROM THE SUN

SUPPLY LIST

Ping-pong ball   Paint   Basketball, volleyball, or other larger ball
Supplies for Challenge: Modeling Clay   8 pencils   Protractor   Index cards

BEGINNERS

- What is the name of the seventh planet from the sun? **Uranus.**
- What color is Uranus? **Pale blue.**
- How does Uranus move that is different from other planets? **It rolls around the sun instead of spinning upright.**

WHAT DID WE LEARN?

- What makes Uranus unusual compared to the other planets? **It rotates on its side.**
- How have rings been discovered around Uranus? **By telescopes and space probes.**

TAKING IT FURTHER

- How can we learn more about Uranus? **Send out more probes; build better telescopes.**
- Why is Uranus such a cold planet? **It is too far from the sun for the sun to heat it very much.**

LESSON 26 · NEPTUNE

LAST OF THE GAS GIANTS

SUPPLY LIST

Flashlight   3 clear plastic or glass cups   Red and blue food color
Supplies for Challenge: String   Washer

BEGINNER

- What is the name of the eighth planet from the sun? **Neptune.**
- What color is Neptune? **Blue.**
- Is Neptune a solid or a gas planet? **Gas.**

WHAT DID WE LEARN?

- What similarities are there between Uranus and Neptune? **They are both gas planets and have rings and moons. They both have methane in their atmospheres that make them appear blue. They were both discovered in the last 250 years.**
- What are two possible explanations for the Great Dark Spot? **Some scientists believe it was a giant windstorm in Neptune's atmosphere, others believe it may have been a hole in the clouds surrounding the planet.**

TAKING IT FURTHER

- Explain how Neptune was discovered. **Observations of Uranus's orbit indicated that there must be a planet whose gravity was affecting Uranus. Astronomers/mathematicians calculated where the unknown planet had to be and another astronomer found it there.**
- What affects the color of a planet? **Many things can affect what color a planet appears to be. Mars is red because of the rust (iron oxide) in its soil; earth appears blue because of the water on the surface and its atmosphere; Uranus and Neptune appear blue because of the methane in their atmospheres.**

LESSON 27

PLUTO & ERIS

PLUTOIDS

SUPPLY LIST

Copy of "How Much Do I Weigh?" worksheet   Calculator   Bathroom scale

BEGINNER

- Is Pluto considered a true planet? **No, it is now classified as a plutoid.**
- What is the temperature like on Pluto? **Very cold.**
- How many known moons does Pluto have? **Three.**
- What is the name of the largest moon orbiting Pluto? **Charon.**

WHAT DID WE LEARN?

- What was the last planet to be discovered in our solar system? **Pluto; there may be one or more planets farther out than Pluto.**
- How does the gravity on Pluto compare to the gravity on earth? **There is practically no gravity on Pluto. It is 0.08 times the gravity on earth.**
- Is Pluto always farther away from the sun than Neptune? **No, it is closer to the sun than Neptune for 20 out of every 250 years.**
- What is unique about how Charon orbits Pluto? **They are in a synchronous orbit—the same sides of the planet and moon always face each other**.

TAKING IT FURTHER

- Why did it take so long to discover Pluto? **It's a small planet and very far away. It was much dimmer than expected**.
- Why is Pluto no longer considered to be a planet? **It is too small; it does not meet the definition for a planet adopted by the International Astronomical Union.**
- What alternate classification was given to Pluto in 2008? **It was called a plutoid.**

QUIZ

4 PLANETS

LESSONS 19–27

Planet	Terrestrial or Jovian	Atmosphere (Yes/No) If yes, what is it made of?	# of known moons	Rings (Yes/No)	Surface temp (Hot/Cold/ Comfortable)
Mercury	**Terrestrial**	**Not much—very thin helium/hydrogen**	**0**	**No**	**Hot and cold**
Venus	**Terrestrial**	**Yes—carbon dioxide/ nitrogen/sulfuric acid**	**0**	**No**	**Hot**
Earth	**Terrestrial**	**Yes—nitrogen/oxygen**	**1**	**No**	**Comfortable**
Mars	**Terrestrial**	**Yes—carbon dioxide**	**2**	**No**	**Comfortable to cold**
Jupiter	**Jovian**	**Yes—hydrogen**	**60+**	**Yes**	**Cold**
Saturn	**Jovian**	**Yes—hydrogen/helium**	**30+**	**Yes**	**Cold**
Uranus	**Jovian**	**Yes—hydrogen/helium/ methane**	**20+**	**Yes**	**Cold**
Neptune	**Jovian**	**Yes—hydrogen/helium/ methane**	**13**	**Yes**	**Cold**
Pluto (plutoid)	**Neither/ unknown**	**Possibly/Sometimes— very thin methane**	**3**	**No**	**Cold**

CHALLENGE QUESTIONS

• **Mercury—has a slight atmosphere, has a magnetic field, is similar to our moon; Venus—surface geography, temperature and pressure; Earth—not needed; Mars—Soil composition, surface geography, possible water ice; Jupiter—information on Great Red Spot; Saturn—shepherd moons, Enceladus's role in ring formation; Uranus and Neptune—discovery of moons; Pluto—none yet.**

SPACE PROGRAM

LESSON 28

NASA

THE NATIONAL AERONAUTICS AND SPACE ADMINISTRATION

SUPPLY LIST

Tagboard/poster board   Steel BBs   Magnet   Plastic lid or dish   Several books

BEGINNERS

- What is NASA? **The National Aeronautics and Space Administration—a group of people who work on different ways to study space.**

- Name three ways that NASA studies things in space. **Launching rockets, Space Shuttle, Space Station, Hubble Telescope, by conducting experiments, and training astronauts.**

- What was the first important job that NASA had to do? **Find a way to send a man to the moon.**

WHAT DID WE LEARN

- What is NASA? **The National Aeronautics and Space Administration, a science organization for studying the universe.**

- When was NASA formed? **1958.**

- What was one of NASA's first tasks? **To put a man on the moon.**

- List at least three of NASA's work groups. **Improving aeronautics, space flight, space probes, robotics, space station, analyzing data, planning missions.**

TAKING IT FURTHER

- How does NASA help people who are not interested in space exploration? **By developing technology that is applicable in other areas.**

- How might an evolutionary worldview affect NASA's work? **Many of NASA's projects are dedicated to finding life on Mars or other planets/moons; others are designed to prove the Big Bang. If NASA had a biblical worldview, their missions could be discovering the wonders of the universe that glorify God.**

CHALLENGE: NACA

- What was NACA? **National Advisory Committee for Aeronautics.**

- What was its original purpose? **To supervise and direct the scientific study of the problems of flight, with a view to their practical solution.**

- What were some of the major contributions to aeronautics that were made by NACA? **Supersonic and hypersonic flight technology, safety designs, improved engines, airfoils, and wings.**

LESSON 29

SPACE EXPLORATION

SEEING WHAT'S OUT THERE

SUPPLY LIST

Styrofoam balls   Toothpicks   Empty thread spools   Aluminum foil   Modeling clay
Tagboard/poster board   Model rocket and launch pad (optional)
Supplies for Challenge: Drawing materials

BEGINNERS

- What is a satellite? **Something that orbits the earth.**

- What is a space probe? **Something sent to other planets to take pictures and get other information.**

- What invention was needed in order to send satellites and other items into space? **Rockets.**

WHAT DID WE LEARN?

- Who were the first people to talk about going into space? **The science fiction writers of the 19th century.**

- Who is considered the father of modern rocketry? **Robert H. Goddard.**

- What major event sparked interest in the development of the rocket for space travel? **The extensive use of rockets during World War II.**

- Who was one of the primary developers of rockets in the United States after World War II? **The German scientist, Werner VonBraun.**

- What was the first man-made object to orbit the earth? **Sputnik—a satellite launched by the Soviet Union.**

- Who was the first man in space? **Yuri Gagarin.**

- Who was the first American in space? **Alan Shepherd.**

- Who was the first American to orbit the earth? **John Glenn.**

- Who was the first man to walk on the moon? **Neil Armstrong.**

TAKING IT FURTHER

- Why are satellites an important part of space exploration? **Satellites have many purposes including collecting scientific and military data, communications, and navigation.**

- Why are space probes an important part of space exploration? **Probes can go to places that are too far away for humans to travel and places that are too dangerous for humans. The atmosphere on Venus crushed several of the early probes that were sent there. Losing a probe is a risk worth taking, but risking human life is not. Most of the information we have about the other planets has come from space probes.**

LESSON 30

APOLLO PROGRAM

FIRST FLIGHT TO THE MOON

SUPPLY LIST

String (enough to reach across a room)   2 balloons   2 straws   Tape

BEGINNERS

- What was the name of the project that sent men to the moon? **Apollo.**
- How many stages or rocket engines did the Saturn V rocket have? **Three.**
- Who were the first men on the moon? **Neil Armstrong and Buzz Aldrin.**

WHAT DID WE LEARN?

- What was the name of the NASA program whose goal was to put a man on the moon? **Apollo.**
- What are the three modules in the Apollo spacecraft? **The command module, the service module, and the lunar module.**
- What were the two parts of the lunar module designed to do? **The descent stage allowed astronauts to land on the moon. The ascent stage lifted them from the moon back to the command module in lunar orbit.**
- What was the name of the three-stage rocket used with the Apollo spacecraft? **Saturn V.**

TAKING IT FURTHER

- What is the advantage of a multi-stage rocket engine? **The first engine must lift all of the weight of the combined system, but the second engine only needs to lift the weight of the system after the first stage is gone, so it does not need to be as big. The third stage is only needed to break the modules out of earth's orbit, so it can be relatively small.**

LESSON 31

THE SPACE SHUTTLE

REUSABLE PARTS

SUPPLY LIST

Copy of "Space Shuttle" worksheet

BEGINNERS

- What is the space shuttle? **A reusable space ship for orbiting the earth.**
- What are the three parts of the space shuttle system? **The orbiter, the fuel tank, and the solid rocket boosters.**
- What piece of equipment is in the payload bay that is helpful to astronauts? **A robotic arm.**

SPACE SHUTTLE WORKSHEET

See drawing in student manual, page 137.

WHAT DID WE LEARN?

- What is the main advantage of the space shuttle vehicle over all previous manned space vehicles? **The shuttle is reusable, thus it is much less expensive to operate.**

- What are the main purposes of the shuttle program? **Scientific experiments, launching of space satellites, and ferrying astronauts and supplies to the space station.**

- What are the two main parts of the orbiter and what are their purposes? **The crew cabin contains the flight deck and living areas. The payload bay provides room for satellites and experiments. It also provides an area where repair work can be done**.

TAKING IT FURTHER

- Why is the space shuttle called an orbiter? **It is designed to orbit the earth for experimental purposes. It is not designed for outer space flight.**

- Why is the orbiter shaped like an airplane? **The shape of a space vehicle is relatively unimportant in space because there is no gravity and no atmosphere. However, the shuttle must be able to land safely on earth. So it is designed with aerodynamics similar to an airplane, so it can land like a plane in the earth's atmosphere.**

- Why does the orbiter have to be carried back to Florida if it lands in California? **The shuttle does not have any jet engines or any way to propel itself through the atmosphere. It only has booster engines that allow it to move in space. So, although it may resemble an airplane, it can't fly like one.**

LESSON 32 INTERNATIONAL SPACE STATION

REACHING FOR FREEDOM

SUPPLY LIST

Water   Waxed paper   Toothpick

BEGINNERS

- What is the name of the current space station? **International Space Station.**

- How does the space station get power? **From large solar panels that convert the sun's energy into electricity.**

- Why can astronauts do different experiments on the space station than on earth? **There is very little gravity on the space station**.

WHAT DID WE LEARN?

- What is the International Space Station? **A permanent orbiting laboratory in space.**

- Why do countries feel there is a need for a space station? **To study long-term effects of micro-gravity for scientific purposes and to develop new technologies to benefit all of humanity.**

TAKING IT FURTHER

- What shape would you expect a flame to be on the space station? **A candle flame is somewhat teardrop shaped on earth. However, in space it is circular because the oxygen molecules are equally available from all directions and are not being pulled down by gravity.**

LESSON 33

ASTRONAUTS

MODERN DAY EXPLORERS

SUPPLY LIST

Winter clothing including hat, gloves, coat, snow pants, and boots   Hand mirror
Building blocks   Nut and bolt   Optional: Bicycle helmet or motorcycle helmet with face mask
Supplies for Challenge: Research materials on astronauts

BEGINNERS

- What are two important subjects to study in school if you want to become an astronaut? **Math and science.**

- What things do space suits provide that are missing in space? **Air, air pressure, water, heating and cooling, the ability to communicate.**

- How does an astronaut move around in space? **With a rocket pack.**

WHAT DID WE LEARN?

- What are some ways that astronauts train for their missions? **They learn about the vehicles they will be using and the experiments they will be performing. They practice in their spacesuits underwater. They ride in the "Vomit Comet."**

- What conditions in space require astronauts to need spacesuits? **There is no atmosphere in space so there is no pressure, no oxygen, and no protection from the hot and cold extremes in space. Also, there is more radiation in space so extra protection is needed.**

TAKING IT FURTHER

- What are some things you can do if you want to become an astronaut? **Study math and science, keep physically fit, and work hard.**

- What would you like to do if you were involved in the space program? **Answers will vary.**

QUIZ 5

SPACE PROGRAM

LESSONS 28–33

Choose the best answer for each question.

1. _**B**_ At this time, what is the best way to study long-term effects of zero-gravity?

2. _**A**_ Which characteristic is generally not a quality of an astronaut?

3. _**D**_ What was designed to protect astronauts in space?

4. _**C**_ What wartime invention led to space exploration?

5. _**A**_ What object was launched into space on Oct. 4, 1957?

6. _**B**_ Who was the first man in space?

7. _**C**_ Who challenged America to put a man on the moon before 1970?

8. _**A**_ Which of the following is not a function of space satellites?

9. _**D**_ Which of the following programs did not help to put a man on the moon?

10. _**B**_ What rocket was used in the Apollo space program?

11. _**C**_ Who was the first person to walk on the moon?

12. _**C**_ Which of the following was not left on the moon?

13. _**D**_ What shape is the shuttle orbiter?

14. _**B**_ What is the maximum number of crew members on the space shuttle?

CHALLENGE QUESTIONS

Short answer:

15. List three ways that NACA helped improve flight. **Improved air foils, engines, and wings, safety improvements, ice reduction processes, hypersonic and supersonic designs.**

16. List three challenges unique to living and working in space. **No gravity, no air, no air pressure, no heat and cold protection, radiation.**

17. Why is private space research important? **Competition spurs innovation; commercial applications will help support further research; improvements in space research can be applied to other areas of life; private space research looks at areas that are not funded by the government so improvements are made in more areas.**

18. List two differences between the space shuttle and the Orion. **Shuttle is shaped like a plane while Orion is shaped like a capsule; shuttle is only an orbiter while Orion will be able to go to the moon; shuttle can land on an airstrip while Orion must land in the water.**

19. List two ways that the space shuttle and the Orion are similar. **Both are reusable; both can take people to and from the space station; both can launch satellites.**

20. What is one fascinating thing you have learned? **Answers will vary.**

LESSON 34 · SOLAR SYSTEM MODEL: FINAL PROJECT

SHOWING WHAT'S OUT THERE

FINAL PROJECT SUPPLY LIST

Styrofoam balls in the following sizes: 5 in. (1 each)   4 in. (1 each)   3 in. (1 each)
2½ in. (1 each)   2 in. (1 each)   1½ in. (2 each)   1¼ in. (2 each)
2 Styrofoam 4½-inch rings   5 stiff craft wires—each 14 inches long   Paint
Supplies for Challenge: Index cards

What did we learn?

- What holds all of the planets in orbit around the sun? **The force of gravity.**
- What other items are in our solar system that are not included in your model? **Asteroids, comets, meteoroids, Pluto and other plutoids.**

Taking it further

- Why do the planets orbit the sun and not the earth? **The sun is the most massive object in the solar system. It therefore has the strongest gravitational pull so smaller items, such as planets, will orbit it.**

FINAL EXAM

OUR UNIVERSE

LESSONS 1–34

Fill in the blank with the correct term from below.

1. An _**asteroid**_ is a chunk of rock in a regular orbit around the sun.
2. The surface of the moon is covered with dark areas called _**maria**_.
3. A piece of space debris that burns up in the earth's atmosphere is a _**meteor**_.
4. Space _**probes**_ can explore areas that man cannot.
5. A piece of space debris that hits the earth's surface is a _**meteorite**_.
6. A _**supernova**_ is a star that experiences a very large explosion.
7. A _**comet**_ is a ball of ice and dust that orbits the sun.
8. A star that has exploded and collapsed in on itself is called a _**black hole**_.
9. An _**eclipse**_ occurs when one heavenly body blocks the light from another heavenly body.
10. The gases surrounding a planet are its _**atmosphere**_.
11. A large cloud of gas and dust in space is a _**nebula**_.
12. Heated plasma that extends from the surface of the sun to 6,200 miles is the _**chromosphere**_.
13. The _**corona**_ is the outermost part of the sun's atmosphere.
14. The visible surface of the sun is called the _**photosphere**_.
15. _**Solar energy**_ is energy from the sun.
16. A _**satellite**_ is anything that has a regular orbit around a planet.

Short answer:

17. List at least one unique characteristic for each planet (or plutoid). **Accept any reasonable answer.**

    Mercury—Closest to the sun, little or no atmosphere, no moons, extreme temperatures.

    Venus—Sulfuric acid clouds, hottest planet in the solar system, closest in size to earth.

    Earth—Only planet with life, significant amount of water, designed by God for us.

    Mars—Red planet, frozen carbon dioxide at the poles, most space probes.

    Jupiter—Largest planet, Great Red Spot, gas giant.

    Saturn—Beautiful rings, second largest planet, gas giant.

    Uranus—Rotates on its side, blue color.

    Neptune—Methane atmosphere gives it a blue color, had the Great Dark Spot.

Pluto—Former planet, classified as a plutoid, Charon in synchronous orbit.

18. Describe why gravity is important to our solar system. **Gravity holds everything in place. It makes the planets orbit the sun. It makes the moons orbit the planets. It holds our atmosphere in place.**

19. Place these colors of stars in order from coolest to hottest: blue, orange, yellow, white: **Orange, yellow, white, blue.**

20. What are the two ways that planets move through space? **Rotate on axes, revolve around the sun.**

21. List three tools used to study space. **Space probe, space ships/shuttle, space station, satellite, telescopes.**

22. What was the purpose of the Apollo missions? **To send a man to the moon.**

23. Why was the space shuttle developed? **To make a reusable space ship, to do research in orbit.**

24. What is the purpose of the International Space Station? **To have a place to conduct long-term micro-gravity experiments.**

25. List three purposes of a space suit. **To protect the astronaut from harmful radiation and extreme temperature, to provide pressure and air, to provide communications.**

CHALLENGE QUESTIONS

Mark each statement as either True or False.

26. _T_ A Foucault pendulum demonstrates the rotation of the earth.

27. _F_ Kepler was the first to suggest the heliocentric model of the universe.

28. _F_ Distant starlight proves the universe is billions of years old.

29. _T_ The celestial equator on a star map corresponds to the equator on a map of the earth.

30. _T_ Sir Isaac Newton improved on Galileo's design of the early telescope.

31. _T_ The larger the opening of a telescope, the more you can magnify the image.

32. _T_ Hektor and Achilles are two asteroids in the Trojan asteroid family.

33. _F_ Science has proven that a meteor led to the extinction of the dinosaurs.

34. _T_ Kepler's laws of planetary motion explain why planets move in ellipses.

35. _F_ Solar flares are unrelated to sunspots.

36. _F_ All planets are at the same tilt with respect to the sun.

37. _T_ There are four Jovian and four terrestrial planets.

38. _T_ Mercury and Venus have very different atmospheres from earth.

39. _T_ More space probes have gone to Mars than to any other planet.

40. _F_ SpaceShipOne proved that private space research is unrealistic.

41. _T_ Orion is being modeled after the Apollo program.

42. _F_ Only official astronauts are allowed on the International Space Station.

43. _T_ Most astronauts have had a military background.

CONCLUSION

REFLECTING ON OUR UNIVERSE

SUPPLY LIST

Bible   Flashlight   Blanket   Night sky

WHAT DID WE LEARN?

- What is the best thing you learned about our universe? **Answers will vary.**

OUR PLANET EARTH

UNIT 1
ORIGINS & GLACIERS

LESSON 1

INTRODUCTION TO EARTH SCIENCE

THE STUDY OF OUR WORLD

SUPPLY LIST

Tennis ball   String   Masking tape

BEGINNERS

- What is earth science? **The study of the earth.**
- Where did the earth come from? **God created it.**
- What other things did God create? **The sun, moon, stars, sky, land, plants, animals, people.**

WHAT DID WE LEARN?

- What are the four main studies of earth science? **Space/astronomy, atmosphere/meteorology, lithosphere/geology, and water/hydrology.**
- What is one question mentioned in this lesson that science cannot answer about the earth? **Where it came from originally. There are many other questions beyond science as well.**
- Why can we rely on God's Word to tell us where the earth came from? **The Bible is the Word of God and God does not lie. The evidence around us confirms what the Bible says.**

TAKING IT FURTHER

- How does the First law of thermodynamics confirm the Genesis account of creation? **Since matter cannot be created by natural means, then a supernatural event must have occurred to make that material. The Bible says God spoke it into existence.**
- How does the Second law of thermodynamics confirm the Genesis account of creation? **If the whole universe is slowing down and losing energy, there must have been a time when everything was started, the energy was put into the whole system. Together with the First Law, this shows that a supernatural event, such as the creation described in the Bible, must have happened in the past.**
- Read Psalm 139:8–10. What do these verses say about where we can find God? **God is present everywhere, even in space or at the bottom of the ocean; wherever we go, God is with us.**

INTRODUCTION TO GEOLOGY

THE STUDY OF THE EARTH ITSELF

SUPPLY LIST

Copy of "Geology Scavenger Hunt"

Supplies for Challenge: "Periodic Table of the Elements"(page 15 in student manual)

Packaged food with nutrition labels

BEGINNERS

- What is geology? **The study of the earth.**

- What makes earth a special planet? **It has lots of water, is the right distance from the sun.**

- What are some things around you that came from the earth? **Anything made from metal, plastic, or rock. Anything made from plants because they grow in the soil.**

GEOLOGY SCAVENGER HUNT

1. Milk	2. Toothpaste	3. Salt	4. Cereal
5. Pencils	6. Chalk	7. Matches	8. Baby powder
9. Rechargable batteries	10. Drywall	11. Computer chips	12. Pennies
13. Electrical wiring	14. Thermometer	15. Paper clip or staple	

WHAT DID WE LEARN?

- What is geology? **The study of the earth and the processes that affect it.**

- What are some of the evidences that God designed the earth uniquely to support life? **The abundance of water and its properties, just the right amount of oxygen in the atmosphere, the distance of the earth from the sun, the tilt of the earth.**

TAKING IT FURTHER

- List some ways that geology affects your life on a regular basis. **Minerals and metals are in nearly every object around you. You use gas in your car. Your house must be built on a firm foundation.**

- What area of geology interests you the most? **Go to the library and learn more about it.**

CHALLENGE: ELEMENTS

- **You are likely to find sodium, potassium, phosphorus, magnesium, zinc, copper, iron, and calcium.**

LESSON 3

THE EARTH'S HISTORY

HOW IT ALL BEGAN

SUPPLY LIST

Jar with lid   Rocks, pebbles, sand, dirt   Water

BEGINNERS

- What are the three important events that made the earth the way it is today? **Creation, Fall, Flood.**

- Does the Bible say that the earth is thousands or billions of years old? **The Bible says thousands of years.**

WHAT DID WE LEARN?

- What are the two most popular views for how the earth became what it is today? **Creation/biblical and evolution/uniformitarian.**

- According to the Bible, what are the three major events that affected the way the earth looks today? **Creation, the Fall of man, the Flood.**

- Should a good scientist disregard evidence that contradicts his/her ideas? **No, he/she should examine the evidence and try to understand why it does not agree. Sometimes the answer cannot be found now, but may be obvious later, when other discoveries are made.**

- Have scientists proven that evolution is true? **No! Evolution is a model of origins that cannot be proven, and actually contradicts what we observe. A historical event, such as the origin of the world, cannot be recreated or tested, so it cannot be proven. We must trust the account of the One who was there—God.**

- Have scientists proven that biblical creation is true? **No. Creation and evolution both deal with historical events—origins science. Neither can be proven by science. But, when the evidence is examined, it contradicts the evolutionary view and confirms the Bible's account.**

TAKING IT FURTHER

- How might scientists explain the discovery of fossilized seashells in the middle of a desert? **An ocean must have covered the desert at one time. The Bible says the whole world was covered with water during the Flood. Evolutionists say the climate was very different in the past, causing the oceans to cover more of the world.**

- Explain how a fossilized tree could be found upright through several layers of rock. **The tree had to have been covered with the various layers before it had a chance to decay. This must have occurred relatively quickly, over a few years time, not over millions of years. In fact, we see an example where hundreds of trees are settling upright into sediment at the bottom of Spirit Lake following the 1980 eruption of Mount St. Helens.**

LESSON 4

THE GREAT FLOOD

GOD'S PUNISHMENT FOR SIN

SUPPLY LIST

Paper   Drawing materials (colored pencils, markers, etc.)

Supplies for Challenge: Copy of "Did the Flood Really Happen?" worksheet

BEGINNERS

- Why did God send the Genesis Flood? **To punish man's wickedness.**
- How did the Flood affect the surface of the earth? **It laid down layers of mud that formed new rocks, and fossils, and it washed away areas of the earth.**
- How was the weather different after the Flood? **It was probably much cooler.**

WHAT DID WE LEARN?

- What are some things geologists observe that point to a worldwide Flood? **Large amounts of sedimentary rock, abundant fossils, most fossils are aquatic.**
- What major geological events may have been associated with the Flood of Noah's day? **Major volcanic activity, separation of the landmasses, the Ice Age, formation of mountain ranges.**

TAKING IT FURTHER

- How would a huge flood change the way the earth looks? **Rushing water would cause massive erosion, wearing away rock. This would cause valleys to form and would move rock and soil from one place to another. It would also bury massive amounts of plants and animals under thick layers of mud resulting in abundant fossils, as well as coal and oil deposits.**
- Why did God send a huge flood? **To punish man for his wickedness.**

CHALLENGE: DID THE FLOOD REALLY HAPPEN? WORKSHEET

1. _**Yes**_ Water would wash away rocks, soil, and buildings.
2. _**Yes**_ Millions of animals and people would die.
3. _**Yes**_ The water would move rocks and soil from one place to another.
4. _**Yes**_ Buildings would be destroyed.
5. _**No**_ Land would be unchanged.
6. _**Yes**_ A large boat would float on the water.
7. _**Yes**_ Land animals would be covered with mud and sand.
8. _**Yes**_ Debris would settle out of the water.
9. _**No**_ Plants would not be uprooted or killed.
10. _**Yes**_ New paths would be formed for water to flow through.

With this in mind, list at least three things that you would expect to find, hundreds or even thousands of years later when you dig into the earth.

- **Millions of fossils—mostly of sea creatures found all over the world.**

- Fossils of sea creatures on the tops of high mountains.
- Fossils of sea creatures in the middle of deserts.
- Oil and coal that were formed from dead plants and sea creatures that were buried under tons of rock.
- Layers of sedimentary rock.
- Some rock layers are curved or folded as if they were all soft at the same time.
- Deep canyons were carved.

These are just a few evidences that support the idea of a worldwide flood.

LESSON 5

THE GREAT ICE AGE

THE AGE OF WOOLY MAMMOTHS

SUPPLY LIST

Copy of "Ice Age Crossword Puzzle"

Supplies for Challenge: Copy of world map   World Atlas with climate map of world

BEGINNERS

- How did the weather after the Flood compare to the weather before the Flood? **The weather was probably much cooler.**
- What could make the weather cooler after the Flood? **More clouds and more ash from volcanoes.**
- Was the earth completely covered with ice during the Ice Age? **No, much of the earth was still warm and people lived there.**

ICE AGE CROSSWORD PUZZLE

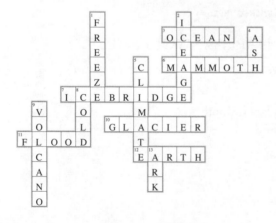

WHAT DID WE LEARN?

- What two conditions are necessary for an ice age? **Wetter winters and cooler summers.**
- How did the Genesis Flood set up conditions for a great ice age? **Warm oceans allowed for lots of evaporation and therefore lots of snow. Volcanic ash blocked much of the sunlight, causing much cooler summers.**

- How do evolutionists explain the needed conditions for multiple ice ages? **They cannot adequately explain what causes the additional moisture or the cooler temperatures.**

TAKING IT FURTHER

- Do we see new glaciers forming today? **We see some new glaciers forming and some old glaciers growing bigger for a few years, but not on the large scale they did during the Ice Age.**

LESSON
6

GLACIERS

ICE THAT NEVER MELTS

SUPPLY LIST

Several ice cubes   Dish of water   Toy boat that will fit in the dish

BEGINNERS

- What is a glacier? **A sheet of ice that does not completely melt even in the summer.**
- Where are most glaciers located? **At the North and South Poles.**
- Where do icebergs come from? **They are large pieces of ice that have broken off of glaciers and fallen into the water.**

WHAT DID WE LEARN?

- What is a glacier? **A formation of ice that does not completely melt from year to year.**
- How does a glacier form? **The snow accumulates each year because it does not completely melt during the summer. The weight of the snow compacts the snow below it, eventually turning it to ice.**
- What are the three types of glaciers? **Valley—forms in a valley, Piedmont—spreads out from two or more valleys, Continental—forms in a relatively flat area and spreads out in all directions.**
- What is calving? **When glaciers reach water and pieces break off into the water.**

TAKING IT FURTHER

- Why do glaciers exist mostly at the poles and on high mountain tops? **That is where it stays cold enough in the summers to keep the snow and ice from completely melting.**
- Why is it cold enough to prevent glaciers from melting at the North Pole, when there is 20–24 hours of sunlight during the summer? **Even though there are many hours of sunlight, the light hits the earth at a steep angle, so most of the heat is reflected.**

MOVEMENT OF GLACIERS

SLOWLY CREEPING DOWN THE VALLEY

SUPPLY LIST

Empty half-gallon milk carton   Water, sand, and pebbles   Pair of gloves

Note: this activity requires the water to freeze overnight. You may want to start it the day before you do the lesson.

Supplies for Challenge: Glass jar with lid   Newspaper   Plastic zipper bag   Work gloves

BEGINNERS

- What makes a glacier move? **Gravity.**
- What moves along with the ice? **Dirt, rocks, other debris.**
- How can you tell how far a glacier has moved in the past? **Rocks and dirt that were pushed by the glacier are left in a line ahead of the glacier's farthest position.**

WHAT DID WE LEARN?

- What is the shape of a valley carved by glaciers? **U-shaped.**
- How do glaciers pick up rocks and other debris? **They melt, and the water flows around the rocks; then the water refreezes and the rocks become part of the glacier.**
- What is the name of the line of rocks that marks the furthest advance of the glacier? **Terminal moraine.**

TAKING IT FURTHER

- How might a scientist tell how far a glacier moved a rock or boulder? **One way is to test what kind of rock the boulder is made of. Often, it is a different type than the rocks around it. Then, the scientist must trace the path of the glacier backward to where that type of rock is found.**
- Why do glaciers often have deep cracks and crevices? **The lower layers of ice move smoothly while the upper layers, which are less compressed, are more brittle and break rather than move with the glacier.**

QUIZ

1

ORIGINS & GLACIERS

LESSONS 1–7

Mark each statement as either True or False.

1. _T_ We can rely on the Bible to tell us the truth about God and His creation.
2. _F_ We can prove scientifically where the earth came from.
3. _F_ Science can answer all of our questions.
4. _T_ Fossils have been located in every part of the world.
5. _T_ The biblical account of the Flood explains much of what we see on earth.

6. _F_ A scientist should disregard evidence that contradicts his/her theories.

7. _T_ Scientists have not proven evolution to be true.

8. _T_ The abundance of aquatic fossils is consistent with a worldwide Flood.

9. _T_ The worldwide Flood was God's punishment for man's sin.

10. _T_ Evolutionists cannot adequately explain how conditions formed to create an ice age.

Short answer:

11. List three biblical events that greatly affected the surface of the earth. **Creation, Fall, Flood.**

12. Describe three attributes of the earth that make it just right for life to occur here.
Distance from sun, tilt of axis, properties and abundance of water, oxygen/nitrogen ratio, size provides just the right amount of gravity.

13. List three ways that geology affects your life. **Minerals in food, anything made of metal, oil, anything made of plastic, soil to grow plants, caves to explore, etc.**

14. List the two climate conditions required for an ice age. **Wet winters and cool summers.**

15. List the four main studies of earth science. **Astronomy, meteorology, geology, hydrology.**

CHALLENGE QUESTIONS

Short answer:

16. Explain what the following quote is saying about scientists who believe in evolution.

    Dr. Scott Todd, an immunologist at Kansas State University: "Even if all the data point to an intelligent designer, such an hypothesis is excluded from science because it is not naturalistic." **Evolutionists will ignore the data if they point to a Creator.**

17. Based on what you have learned about the great Ice Age, in which areas would you expect to see evidence of glaciers? Write yes if you would expect to see it and no if you would not expect to see it.

    A. _Yes_ Canada   B. _Yes_ Montana   C. _No_ Mexico

    D. _Yes_ Norway   E. _Yes_ Siberia   F. _No_ Egypt

18. List three economic or social effects caused by the Little Ice Age. **Changes in fishing grounds; changes in the crops that could be grown; some people had to move as glaciers advanced; less food was available so some people suffered from famine, etc.**

ROCKS & MINERALS

LESSON 8

DESIGN OF THE EARTH

BLUEPRINT FOR THE PLANET

SUPPLY LIST

1 gumball per child   Bowl   1 large marshmallow per child   Pencil
Chocolate chips   Small bottle or jar   1 toothpick per child   Waxed paper

Supplies for Challenge: Chocolate chips   Plastic zipper bag   Cup   Water

BEGINNERS

- What are the three parts of the earth? **The crust, mantle, and core.**
- What is the hottest part of the earth? **The core.**
- What is the thinnest part of the earth? **The crust.**

WHAT DID WE LEARN?

- What do most scientists believe to be the three main parts of the earth? **The core, the mantle and the crust.**
- Which is the thickest part of the earth? **The mantle.**
- Which is the thinnest part of the earth? **The crust.**
- Where is the crust the thickest? **Under the mountains.**

TAKING IT FURTHER

- Why do scientists believe the mantle is hotter and denser than the crust? **Earthquake or seismic waves travel more quickly through the mantle than through the crust.**
- For what other things, besides the interior of the earth, do scientists have to develop models without actually seeing what they are describing? **Very small things like atoms, very large things like the universe, things they are designing like airplanes or space ships.**

LESSON 9

ROCKS

BOULDERS, ROCKS, GRAVEL, PEBBLES . . .

SUPPLY LIST

Copy of "The Rock Cycle" worksheet

Supplies for Challenge: Several rocks

BEGINNERS

- Where can you find rocks? **Everywhere.**
- What are the three different kinds of rocks? **Igneous, sedimentary, metamorphic.**

THE ROCK CYCLE WORKSHEET

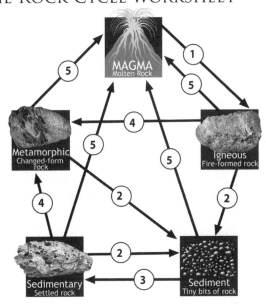

WHAT DID WE LEARN?

- What are rocks made from? **One or more minerals or organic materials.**
- What are the three categories of rocks? **Igneous, sedimentary, and metamorphic.**
- How is igneous rock formed? **Igneous rock forms when melted rock, called magma, cools.**
- How is sedimentary rock formed? **Sedimentary rock forms when layers of sediment are pressed and cemented together in some way.**
- How is metamorphic rock formed? **Metamorphic rock is formed when either igneous or sedimentary rock is exposed to high pressure and high temperature for an extended period of time. The rock's atomic structure is changed and it becomes a different type of rock.**

TAKING IT FURTHER

- Why are rocks important? **They affect nearly every area of our lives.**

- Where is a good place to look for rocks? **You can find rocks nearly everywhere. It depends on what specific kinds of rocks you are looking for. You will more easily find rocks in areas with little or no soil.**

- Why is it better to store your rock samples in a box with dividers than in a bag? **Some rocks are harder than others. In a bag, the samples will hit against each other and may scratch or break each other.**

LESSON 10   IGNEOUS ROCKS

FIRE ROCKS

SUPPLY LIST

Alum   Saucepan   Water   2 craft sticks   2 paper or plastic cups
Supplies for Challenge: Several samples of igneous rocks   Rock and Mineral Guide
Magnifying glass

BEGINNERS

- How is igneous rock formed? **When liquid rock cools it forms igneous rocks.**
- Do crystals grow in rocks that formed inside the earth or on top of the earth? **Inside.**
- What are two uses for igneous rocks? **Monuments and arrow heads.**

WHAT DID WE LEARN?

- What is the difference between magma and lava? **Magma is inside the earth's crust and lava is on top of the earth's crust.**
- How are extrusive rocks formed? **When magma flows to an area where it cools quickly, extrusive rocks are formed. This happens when lava flows to the surface of the earth's crust.**
- How are intrusive rocks formed? **When magma flows to an area inside the crust that is cool enough for it to solidify, but at a slow rate, it forms intrusive rocks.**

TAKING IT FURTHER

- Which kind of igneous rocks have the largest crystals? **The ones that were formed slowly—intrusive rocks.**
- Why is granite commonly used in buildings and monuments? **It is hard and strong, and can be polished.**
- Do all rocks sink in water? **No, pumice often floats.**
- Why not? **Some rocks have air holes in them making them less dense than water, so they float.**
- Where are you likely to find pumice? **Near a previously active volcano.**

SEDIMENTARY ROCKS

LESSON 11

LAYERS OF SEDIMENT

SUPPLY LIST

2 cups of sand   1 cup of cornstarch   Old saucepan   Paint (optional)
Optional: Ingredients to make a peanut butter and jelly or lunchmeat sandwich
Supplies for Challenge: 2 Paper cups   Plaster of Paris   Smooth pebbles
Rough pebbles (like aquarium rocks)   Rock and Mineral Guide

BEGINNERS

- How is a sedimentary rock made in nature? **Water moves bits of rock, sand, or other things around and when they settle they are glued together by chemicals in the water. Then they dry into rocks as the water dries up.**

- When were many of the sedimentary rocks formed? **During the Genesis Flood.**

- Name one common sedimentary rock. **Sandstone, limestone, or man-made rocks such as bricks or sidewalk chalk.**

WHAT DID WE LEARN?

- How are sedimentary rocks formed? **When fragments of rocks and other debris settle out of water they form strata or layers. These layers are pressed together and glued with natural cement to form fragmental sedimentary rock. Chemical rock forms as chemicals precipitate from the water and harden into rock.**

- Were all sedimentary rocks formed during the Flood? **No, but much of the sedimentary rock was probably formed then. New sedimentary rock is still being formed today, especially in caves and other wet areas.**

TAKING IT FURTHER

- Why are fossils found in sedimentary rocks? **Fossils form when plants or animals are covered over with mud or other sediment shortly after dying. Sea creatures were covered over with layers of sediment during the Flood and these layers formed into much of the sedimentary rock we find today. Thus, most of the fossils are found in these rocks.**

- Sediment is simply any small piece of something that settles out of a liquid. What sediment might you find around your house or in nature?
  Coffee grounds, tea leaves and orange juice pulp are a few sediments you might find around your house. Silt is a common sediment found in lakes and ponds. Glaciers melt and leave behind pebbles, rocks and even boulders as sediment.

FOSSILS

HOW DO WE KNOW WHAT DINOSAURS LOOKED LIKE?

SUPPLY LIST

Plaster of Paris   Modeling clay   Petroleum jelly   Cup and spoon
Seashell or other item to "fossilize"

BEGINNERS

- What kinds of animals are most fossils? **Sea creatures such as clams and snails.**

- Why don't most animals become fossils? **Because they are not covered quickly with mud or sand when they die so they quickly decay.**

- What kind of rock contains fossils? **Sedimentary.**

WHAT DID WE LEARN?

- How does an animal become a fossil? **If it is covered by mud, wet sand or other similar substance shortly after is dies, instead of decaying, the hard structures can slowly be replaced by minerals.**

- What are the two different types of fossils? **Cast fossils—imprints; Mold fossils—rock structures in the shape of the original structure.**

- What types of creatures are most fossils? **95% of all fossils are sea invertebrates such as clams and other shellfish.**

TAKING IT FURTHER

- How many true transitional fossils, ones showing one creature evolving into another, have been found? **None!**

- What does this indicate about the theory that land animals evolved from sea creatures? **It shows that there is no physical evidence to support that theory.**

- What are some things we can learn from fossils? **What kinds of plants and animals existed in the past, how those plants and animals were shaped compared to species that exist today, and what plants and animals are now extinct.**

- What kinds of things cannot be learned from fossils? **Usually soft structures such as noses, hair, etc. are not preserved, so it is hard to tell exactly what a creature looked like. You can't tell its color either. Also, if only one or two bones are found, it is very difficult to know with certainty what that creature looked like. Some characteristics can be implied from fossil evidence but cannot be proven. For example, many scientists believe that at least some of the dinosaurs were warm-blooded because the distance between fossilized footprints indicates they must have been able to move quickly—an ability usually limited to warm-blooded creatures. However, this characteristic cannot be proven from the fossil evidence alone.**

LESSON 13

FOSSIL FUELS

A MAJOR ENERGY SOURCE

SUPPLY LIST

2 sponges   Epsom salt   Shallow dish or pan   Scissors   Food coloring (optional)

Supplies for Challenge: Copy of "What Would You Expect?" worksheet

BEGINNERS

- What are the three types of fossil fuels? **Coal, oil, natural gas.**
- What is coal made from? **Plants.**
- What is oil made from? **Sea creatures.**
- What do we use fossil fuels for? **To generate electricity, to make gasoline for our cars, to heat our homes, etc.**

WHAT DID WE LEARN?

- What is the definition of a fossil fuel? **Fuel that was formed from dead plants or animals that were changed by heat and pressure over time.**
- What three forms of fossil fuels do we commonly use? **Coal, oil/petroleum, and natural gas.**

TAKING IT FURTHER

- What evidence supports rapid and recent coal formation instead of slow formation millions of years ago? **Carbon-14 dating, in spite of its limitations, supports recent formation. Boulders and delicate fossils in coal beds also show a young age.**
- Why is finding natural gas when drilling into the ground a good indicator that oil is nearby? **Natural gas is believed to be a by-product of oil formation and is often found in the rocks surrounding an oil field.**
- Why is the existence of natural gas an indication that oil was formed only a few thousand years ago? **Natural gas is a by-product of oil production. If the oil was formed millions of years ago, the gas would have escaped through the rocks by now.**

CHALLENGE: WHAT WOULD YOU EXPECT? WORKSHEET

Lowest level	Upper level	Not found
Flies	Pine needles	Palm trees
Fish	Flies	Coconuts
Algae	Deer	Sea shells
Crawdads	Scrub oak	Parrots
Possibly wild flowers and pine needles	Wild flowers	Possibly crows
	Ground squirrel	
	Snakes	
	Rabbits	
	Possibly crows	

Accept reasonable answers.

- Briefly explain why you put the items where you did. **You would not expect to find items that do not naturally live in the Rocky Mountains such as palm trees, coconuts, sea creatures and parrots. Also, birds could possibly fly to safety and may not have been trapped by the eruption. You would expect to find plants and animals that live in and near the lake in a lower level than those that live above the lake, although some items, such as flowers or pine needles may have been pushed or blown down the hill into the lake. Overall you would expect the land plants and animals to be found above the water plants and animals. Similarly, if there was a worldwide Flood that lasted for five months, you would expect the creatures that lived near the bottom of the ocean to be found in lower layers than those that lived in higher land areas.**

LESSON 14 METAMORPHIC ROCKS

LET'S MAKE A CHANGE

SUPPLY LIST

Copy of "Morphing Ice" worksheet   Waxed paper   Sauce pan
Shaved ice (or snow if available)   2 or 3 pieces of different colored taffy or other soft candy

Supplies for Challenge: Copy of "Metamorphic Match" worksheet   Rock and Mineral Guide

BEGINNERS

- What does the word metamorphic mean? **Changed.**
- What does a rock have to experience to become a changed rock? **Heat, pressure, and time.**
- Name one kind of metamorphic rock? **Marble.**

MORPHING ICE WORKSHEET

Heat only: The rock melts and becomes magma Pressure only: The rock breaks into smaller pieces. Time only: Nothing happens to the rock; it remains the same. Heat, pressure, and time: The rock is changed into metamorphic rock as the molecular structure of the rock changes.

WHAT DID WE LEARN?

- What are the three ingredients needed to change igneous or sedimentary rock into metamorphic rock? **Heat, pressure, and time.**
- Why is marble often swirled instead of pure white? **There are often impurities in the limestone deposits that are a different color from the limestone.**

TAKING IT FURTHER

- Why is metamorphic rock often used for sculptures and monuments? **It is usually very hard and durable. Nonfoliated rock has no crystal structure, so smoother edges are possible.**
- Why is metamorphic rock hard and durable? **The heat and pressure rearrange the crystal structure to form very strong bonds.**

CHALLENGE: METAMORPHIC MATCH WORKSHEET

_C_ Granite   _A_ Shale   _D_ Sandstone   _G_ Limestone
_B_ Mica   _F_ Basalt   _E_ Dolerite

LESSON 15

MINERALS

ANIMAL, VEGETABLE, OR MINERAL?

SUPPLY LIST

Copy of "Mineral Scavenger Hunt" worksheet

Supplies for Challenge: Egg carton   48 small rocks or pebbles

BEGINNERS

- How do you know if something is a mineral or not? **A mineral is solid, natural, not alive, has crystals.**
- Name at least three minerals. **Salt, sugar, silver, gold, copper, zinc, calcium, iron.**

MINERAL SCAVENGER HUNT WORKSHEET

1. Water: **Is not a solid.**
2. Steel: **Is man-made.**
3. Coal: **Is organic (made from plants).**
4. Cookies: **Are mixtures made from varying amounts of minerals.**
5. Glass: **Does not have a crystalline structure.**
- **Minerals around my house include: Calcium in your milk, iron in nails, talc in powder, zinc in your breakfast cereal and fluoride in your toothpaste, etc.**

WHAT DID WE LEARN?

- What five requirements must a substance meet in order to be classified as a mineral? **Naturally occurring, inorganic, constant chemical proportions, regular structure and solid.**
- What is a native mineral? **A mineral that has only one type of atom—a pure element.**
- What is a compound? **A substance with two or more elements in fixed proportions.**

TAKING IT FURTHER

- Are there any minerals that are mixtures? **No, mixtures do not have fixed proportions.**
- What is the difference between a rock and a mineral? **Most minerals are compounds and most rocks are mixtures. Also, rocks can have organic compounds and minerals do not.**
- Is coal a mineral? **No, it is an organic compound. It is a rock.**
- Are all minerals considered rocks? **In their naturally occurring state, minerals are considered rocks.**
- Are all rocks considered minerals? **No, most rocks are made of more than one kind of mineral.**
- Where are you likely to find minerals? **Just about everywhere, such as in your body, your food, toothpaste, coins, cars, radios, TVs, etc.**

LESSON 16

IDENTIFYING MINERALS

IS IT SALT OR SUGAR?

SUPPLY LIST

Copy of "Mineral Identification" worksheet   Magnifying glass   Eye protection/goggles
Samples of 3 or 4 minerals (quartz, feldspar, mica, limestone, etc.)   Masking tape   Penny
Hammer   Old drinking glass   Old pillowcase or towel   Unglazed ceramic tile
Rocks and Minerals Guide
Supplies for Challenge: Copy of "Is it a Rock or a Mineral?" worksheet   Rocks and Minerals Guide

BEGINNERS

- What are three things you can look for to help you identify a rock or mineral? **Color, luster, and crystals.**

WHAT DID WE LEARN?

- What are some common tests used to identify minerals? **Color, streak, luster, crystal shape, hardness, cleavage.**

- Why is color alone not a sufficient test? **Many minerals have the same color. Also, the outside of a sample may change color when exposed to air or water.**

TAKING IT FURTHER

- Is crystal size a good test for identifying a mineral? Why or why not? **No, the size of the crystals is dependent on the temperature at which the sample formed, but is not as dependent on the type of material. Crystal shape is a much better test.**

- What is the difference between cleavage and fracture? **Cleavage indicates that a sample breaks smoothly in one or more directions—showing that the crystal structure is lined up in that direction. Fracture indicates that a sample breaks in smooth curves but not in straight lines.**

- Why do some tests need to be done in a laboratory? **Some tests are too dangerous to do at home and others require special equipment.**

- How can you tell a sample of sugar from a sample of salt? **You could taste the samples to determine which is sugar and which is salt if you are certain they are table salt and sugar. However, you should never taste an unknown sample. A better way would be to use a magnifying glass and observe the shape of the crystals. Salt crystals are usually perfect cubes and sugar crystals are longer and rectangular.**

CHALLENGE: IS IT A ROCK OR A MINERAL? WORKSHEET

Item	Element, compound, or mixture?	What are its main components?	Rock or mineral?
Gold	**Element**	**Gold**	**Mineral**
Granite	**Mixture**	**Quartz, feldspar, and mica,**	**Rock**
Feldspar	**Compound**	**Aluminum and silicon**	**Mineral**
Quartz	**Compound**	**Silicon and oxygen**	**Mineral**
Limestone	**Mixture**	**Calcium carbonate and other materials**	**Rock**
Copper	**Element**	**Copper**	**Mineral**

Diamond	Element	Carbon	Mineral
Obsidian	Mixture	Glass containing silica and aluminum	Rock
Gypsum	Compound	Calcium, sulfur and oxygen	Mineral
Shale	Mixture	Clay and mud	Rock

LESSON 17

VALUABLE MINERALS

HOW MUCH FOR AN OUNCE OF GOLD?

SUPPLY LIST

Chocolate chip cookies   Toothpicks

BEGINNERS

- Name four valuable minerals. **Gold, silver, copper, diamonds.**
- What is the hardest mineral? **Diamond.**
- What are some uses for valuable minerals? **Coins, jewelry, wires, film, pipes.**

WHAT DID WE LEARN?

- What are some valuable minerals? **Gold, silver, copper and diamonds.**
- What is a native mineral? **A mineral made from just one kind of element.**
- What are some important uses for gold? **Jewelry, electronics, money.**
- What are some important uses for silver? **Jewelry, flatware, electronics, film processing.**

TAKING IT FURTHER

- Why is diamond considered an exception among minerals? **Minerals are not supposed to contain carbon—they are inorganic. However, diamond is pure crystallized carbon.**
- Diamonds and coal are both made from carbon. What makes them different? **Coal is a relatively soft black rock made from compressed plant material. Diamonds are carbon atoms that have crystallized due to extreme heat and pressure. Most geologists classify coal as a sedimentary rock and diamond as a metamorphic rock, although some geologists classify coal as a metamorphic rock as well.**

LESSON 18

NATURAL & ARTIFICIAL GEMS

CUT STONES

SUPPLY LIST

Copy of "Breastplate" worksheet   Colored pencils, markers, or crayons

Supplies for Challenge: Pictures of various gems   Visit a mineral exhibit at a museum (optional)

BEGINNERS

- What is a gem? **A stone that can be cut or polished to reflect light.**
- What are three common gems? **Diamond, ruby, emerald, sapphire, topaz, amethyst.**
- How are man-made gems different from natural gems? **They are not as strong; they are sometimes made from different materials; they are made by people instead of occurring naturally.**

WHAT DID WE LEARN?

- What is a gem? **A mineral that is valued by people because of its beauty. Usually gems are brightly colored and have perfect cleavage that allows light to reflect through them.**
- How is a gem different from a native mineral? **Native minerals have only one element. Diamonds are gems that are also native minerals. However, most gems are comprised of more than one element.**
- How are artificial rubies made? **By melting the elements that make natural rubies, then allowing the materials to slowly cool and crystallize.**

TAKING IT FURTHER

- What can you guess about the temperatures at which synthetic rubies are formed? **They are formed at high temperatures.**
- Why would rubies be formed at high temperatures? **Recall from lesson 10 that crystals grow larger when cooled more slowly, so rubies would be cooled at high temperatures to form larger crystals.**
- What are some disadvantages of synthetic gems? **They are not as durable; they are not as valuable; they sometimes look different than naturally occurring gems.**
- Why are natural gems worth more money than artificial gems? **Artificial gems are not as durable. Also, price is partially determined by availability. Natural gems are more scarce than artificial gems and are thus more expensive.**

QUIZ
2

ROCKS & MINERALS

LESSONS 8–18

Choose the best answer for each question.

1. _B_ What percentage of all fossils are fossilized dinosaur bones?
2. _A_ What rock is commonly used for buildings and monuments?
3. _C_ Which of the following is required in order for a plant or animal to fossilize?
4. _A_ What rock is made from the same element as diamonds?
5. _B_ Why should we be careful when using the results of Carbon-14 dating?
6. _C_ What is one common characteristic of metamorphic rock?
7. _A_ How many elements are in a native mineral?
8. _B_ What is a common mineral found in the human body?
9. _D_ Which of the following is a native mineral?
10. _D_ How are artificial gems easily identified?

Short answer:

11. Where is the earth's crust the thickest? **Earth's crust is thickest under the mountains.**

12. Name the three types of rocks. Describe how each type is formed and give an example of each.

    A. **Igneous—formed when melted rock cools. Examples: pumice, basalt, obsidian, granite.**

    B. **Sedimentary—formed from small bits of broken rock, shells and other materials that are cemented together, or when minerals precipitate out of water. Examples: sandstone, mudstone, shale, limestone, dolomite.**

    C. **Metamorphic—formed when igneous or sedimentary rocks are changed by pressure and heat over time. Examples: marble, slate, gneiss, quartzite.**

13. List three tests commonly used to identify minerals. **Tests to identify minerals include color, streak, cleavage, hardness, crystal shape, and luster.**

CHALLENGE QUESTIONS

Match the term with its definition.

14. _C_ The most common element in the earth's crust

15. _E_ Most common rock in continental crust

16. _G_ Most common rock in oceanic crust

17. _H_ Holes found in igneous rocks

18. _A_ Rock containing two or more sizes of crystals

19. _I_ Fragmental rock with rounded clasts

20. _B_ Fragmental rock with angular clasts

21. _J_ Fossilized animal dung

22. _D_ Mineral with atoms of only one type

23. _F_ Mineral with two or more elements in definite proportions

24. _L_ Order of rock layers according to evolutionists

25. _K_ Smooth stones found inside fossilized animal bodies

MOUNTAINS & MOVEMENT

LESSON 19

PLATE TECTONICS

SLIP SLIDING AWAY

SUPPLY LIST

Copy of world map (lesson 5)   Scissors   Tracing paper   Tape
Supplies for Challenge: Graham crackers   Creamy peanut butter or frosting
Waxed paper

BEGINNERS

- What are large areas of land called? **Continents.**
- How many continents do scientists think existed before the Flood? **One.**
- What was that continent called? **Rodinia.**

WHAT DID WE LEARN?

- What is plate tectonics? **The theory that the crust is made up of several large floating plates.**
- How many plates do scientists think there are? **13 plates: 6 major, 7 minor.**

TAKING IT FURTHER

- What are some things that are believed to have happened in the past because of the movement of the tectonic plates? **Continents separated by sea-floor spreading, mountains and ocean basins were formed, volcanic activity.**
- What are some things that happen today because of the movement of the tectonic plates? **Earthquakes, volcanic activity, forming of faults and rifts.**

LESSON 20

MOUNTAINS

DON'T MAKE A MOUNTAIN OUT OF A MOLE HILL

SUPPLY LIST

Copy of "Famous Mountains" worksheet

Supplies for Challenge: Copy of world map   Atlas or topographical map of world

BEGINNERS

- What is a mountain? **An area of land that is taller than the land around it.**
- What is the tallest mountain in the world? **Mount Everest.**
- Name one famous mountain range. **Cascades, Sierra Nevadas, Rocky Mountains, Appalachian Mountains.**

FAMOUS MOUNTAINS WORKSHEET

- _C_ Mountains of Ararat
- _E_ Mount Sinai
- _G_ Mount Moriah
- _D_ Mount Carmel
- _F_ Mount of Olives
- _A_ Mount of Transfiguration
- _B_ Mount Horeb (The Mountain of God)

WHAT DID WE LEARN?

- What is a mountain? **A rise in land with steep sides going up to a summit.**
- What is a mountain range? **A series of mountain peaks in a given area.**
- What is the difference between actual height and elevation of a mountain? **Actual height is the difference between the base and summit of a mountain. Elevation is the height of the summit above sea level.**

TAKING IT FURTHER

- Where are the mountains with the highest elevations located? **In the Himalayan Mountain system in the area between India and China.**
- Is a 700 foot rise a mountain or a hill? **It depends on your perspective. In areas with 5,000 foot mountains, a 700 foot rise will probably be called a hill, but in a relatively flat area it may be called a mountain.**

LESSON 21

TYPES OF MOUNTAINS

HOW DID THEY FORM?

SUPPLY LIST

Newspaper or paper towels
Supplies for Challenge: Sponge

BEGINNERS

- Describe three ways that new mountains can be made. **When material is deposited by a volcano or water, when surrounding material is worn away by water or wind, when the earth's crust is pushed on from two sides.**
- What is the likely cause of many of the mountains we see today? **The Genesis Flood.**

WHAT DID WE LEARN?

- How are depositional mountains formed? **Debris such as ash, lava, sand, etc. is deposited over time, eventually forming a mountain.**
- How are erosional mountains formed? **Large amounts of material are eroded away, such as by a flood, leaving behind mountains and valleys.**
- How are fold and fault mountains formed? **Tectonic plates push against each other and the constant force causes rocks in the middle to fold or slip and push up to form mountains.**

TAKING IT FURTHER

Identify each mountain as either depositional, erosional or fold:

- Mount St. Helens: **This is a volcano—depositional.**
- Bryce Canyon: **Area with many flat-topped sandstone mountains—erosional.**
- Sand Dunes National Monument: **Sand deposited by water and wind—depositional.**
- Rocky Mountains: **Large mountain range—fold.**
- Grand Canyon: **Believed to be carved by a flood—erosional.**
- Mount Everest: **Highest mountain on earth—fold.**

LESSON 22

EARTHQUAKES

SHAKE, RATTLE, AND ROLL

SUPPLY LIST

10–20 building blocks
Supplies for Challenge: Three different colors of modeling clay

Beginners

- How often do earthquakes happen? **Several times each day.**
- What is an aftershock? **A smaller earthquake that occurs after a large earthquake.**
- What is a tsunami? **A giant wave that can be triggered by an earthquake.**

Earthquake-proof Buildings

- What might architects do to help make buildings stronger? **Use reinforcing materials like rebar, overlap joints, and use strong materials.**
- What shape of building is more likely to withstand an earthquake? **Short, broad buildings generally do better than tall, narrow designs.**

What did we learn?

- What is believed to be the cause of earthquakes? **Tectonic plates move against each other causing stress or strain on the rocks. When the stress becomes too great, the rocks move quickly, resulting in an earthquake.**
- What is an aftershock? **A smaller quake that occurs after a major earthquake.**
- What name is given to the area on the earth's surface above where an earthquake originates? **Epicenter.**
- What is a fault? **A crack in the earth's crust resulting from an earthquake.**

Taking it further

- How does the type of material affect the speed of the earthquake waves? **Earthquake waves move more quickly through rock and other dense materials. The waves slow down when traveling through sand, mud and liquid rock or magma.**
- How does this change in speed help scientists "see" under the earth's crust? **Scientists can track the speed of earthquake waves under the crust. When the waves change speed, this tells the scientists that the material at that location is a different density. By tracking this, scientists can predict the thickness of the crust and the density of the magma below it.**
- Why are earthquakes in the middle of the ocean so dangerous? **They trigger tsunamis that can kill people hundreds of miles away.**

LESSON 23
DETECTING & PREDICTING EARTHQUAKES

PREDICTING THE "BIG ONE"

Supply list

Shoebox   Rolling pin   Paper   Pencil   Tape
Supplies for Challenge: Copy of world map

Beginners

- What instrument is used to detect earthquakes? **A seismograph.**
- How can people make buildings safer during earthquakes? **Make them stronger so they can withstand the shaking.**

- Can people accurately predict when and where an earthquake will happen? **No, only God knows when and where earthquakes will happen.**

WHAT DID WE LEARN?

- What is the difference between the magnitude and the intensity of an earthquake? **Magnitude measures the actual strength of the earthquake—how strongly it moved the earth; intensity describes the damage done by the earthquake.**

- What are three factors that determine how much damage is done by an earthquake? **Where it occurs, how strong it is, how long it lasts, how the buildings are built.**

- Explain how a seismograph works. **The part with the rotating drum moves with the earth, and the part with the pen or light is attached to a mass that does not move with the earth.**

- What people group was first to record earthquake measurements? **The Chinese about AD 132.**

TAKING IT FURTHER

- What are some ways people have learned to prepare for earthquakes? **Buildings in areas that are prone to earthquakes are designed and built to be able to withstand vibrations. Also, scientists have an extensive network of seismographs and other instruments to detect earthquakes in hopes of giving enough advance warning for people to leave the area, although this has not proven very effective.**

- What should you do if you are in an earthquake? **The best thing to do is get under something strong, like a sturdy table that can protect you from falling debris.**

LESSON 24

VOLCANOES

FIRE MOUNTAINS

SUPPLY LIST

Baking soda   Vinegar   Empty bottle   Newspaper   Tape   Baking sheet
Red food coloring (optional)

Supplies for Challenge: World map from previous lessons   World atlas

BEGINNERS

- What causes a volcano to erupt? **Pressure under the earth from plates rubbing against each other.**
- What is lava? **Melted rock.**
- What can come out of a volcano besides lava? **Ash, cinders, gases, and bombs.**
- What is the "Ring of Fire"? **The area around the Pacific Ocean where most of the volcanoes exist.**

WHAT DID WE LEARN?

- What are the three stages or states of a volcano? **Active, dormant, extinct.**
- Describe the three main parts of a volcano. **Magma chamber—area below crust filled with melted rock; central vent—channel through which magma forces its way to the surface; crater—indented area around the mouth of the volcano where a cone formed by solidified ash and lava has collapsed.**
- Give the name for each of the following items that are emitted from a volcano:

1. Liquid or melted rock: **Lava.**
2. Tiny bits of solid rock: **Ash.**
3. Pieces of rock from 0.2 to 1 inch (0.5–2.5 cm) in diameter: **Cinders.**
4. Blobs of lava that solidify in the air: **Bombs.**
5. Steam and carbon dioxide: **Gases.**

TAKING IT FURTHER

- How might a volcano become active without anyone noticing? **If it is underwater or located in a very remote area.**

- How are volcanoes and earthquakes related? **Both primarily occur where two tectonic plates meet and cause pressure to build up.**

- How certain can we be that a volcano is really extinct? **Not completely. Several volcanoes have become active after being classified as extinct.**

LESSON 25
VOLCANO TYPES

IS THERE MORE THAN ONE?

SUPPLY LIST

Pie pan   Cookie crumbs   ½ gallon of ice cream   Chocolate chips   Chocolate syrup
Supplies for Challenge: Unopened can of soft drink

BEGINNERS

- What kind of mountain is formed when mostly lava comes from a volcano? **Shield.**
- What kind of mountain is formed when mostly ash and cinders come from a volcano? **Cinder cone.**
- What kind of mountain is formed when a volcano alternates between lava and solid material? **Composite.**

WHAT DID WE LEARN?

- What are the three shapes of volcanoes and how is each formed? **Shield—mostly from lava; Cinder cone—mostly from solid debris such as ash and cinders; Composite—alternating between lava and solid matter.**

- Where are most active volcanoes located today? **Along the Ring of Fire around the Pacific Ocean.**

- What are some of the dangers of volcanoes? **Fire, debris, suffocation from gases, mudslides, tsunamis.**

- What are some positive side effects of volcanoes? **Geothermal energy, sulfur deposits, fertile soil, new land, heat vents in the ocean, black sand beaches.**

TAKING IT FURTHER

- How is the formation of black sand beaches different from the formation of white sand beaches? **Black sand is formed when hot lava shatters as it cools very suddenly when reaching the ocean. Most white sand beaches are composed of crushed shells.**

MOUNT ST. HELENS

GOD'S GIFT TO SCIENTISTS

SUPPLY LIST

Copy of "Volcano Word Search"

BEGINNERS

- What happened at Mount St. Helens on May 18, 1980? **It erupted with a huge explosion.**

- How long did it take for 25 feet of layered ash to accumulate after the eruption? **Only one day.**

- What did the flood of mud and water from the volcano do? **It carved a canyon that was 100 feet deep.**

VOLCANO WORD SEARCH

```
A D O P X Y B A E P A H D S H
C O D O R M A N T E R A C T C
E X S N M K L A I O T C A E R
P A H O E H O E A S M A G R O
U U R S I N D R C H A P T U O
C U S U B D U C T I O N P P Q
O A U L I N S I I E E C R T E
M A G M A O M N V L X Y Z I O
P L M K R V Z D E D T U X O P
O S W Q B O A E L I I F F N A
S C L R E T A R C A N P O S T
I T S U I O B O M B C S H I L
T C N E D R N H F R T W K L J
E C A L D E R A E T X N T M I
R W I O P R Q C M I O R S L P
```

WHAT DID WE LEARN?

- Describe some of the ways the data collected at Mount St. Helens is challenging evolutionary thinking. **Canyons formed in only one day, 25 feet (7.6 m) of sedimentary layers laid down in only one day, upright trees on the bottom of Spirit Lake explain "petrified forests."**

TAKING IT FURTHER

- How did the ash from the eruption of Mount St. Helens affect the weather in 1980? **It darkened the skies and cooled the temperatures, not just near the eruption site, but around the world.**

- How could volcanic activity have contributed to the onset of the Ice Age? **Massive amounts of ash in the atmosphere would have blocked out much of the sunlight, causing cooler summers. Cooler temperatures combined with the large amount of water vapor from warm oceans would cause accumulation of snowfall leading to glacier formation.**

MOUNTAINS & MOVEMENT

LESSONS 19–26

Match the term with its definition.

1. _F_ Theory that the crust is composed of several large landmasses
2. _C_ Name given to original landmass
3. _H_ Series of mountain peaks in a given area
4. _I_ Highest mountain peak on earth
5. _E_ Center of earthquake activity
6. _L_ Smaller quakes after a major earthquake
7. _N_ The Richter scale measures this
8. _D_ Instrument for measuring earthquakes
9. _O_ Blobs of lava that harden in the air
10. _B_ A volcano that has not erupted in the past 50 years
11. _M_ A volcano that is not expected to erupt again
12. _G_ Volcano that recently erupted in Washington state
13. _J_ Volcano that had one of the largest eruptions ever
14. _K_ Type of volcano formed from lava and solid material
15. _A_ One tectonic plate sliding under another

CHALLENGE QUESTIONS

Mark each statement as either True or False.

16. _T_ Continental drift is the name given to the movement of tectonic plates.
17. _F_ Rifting occurs when two tectonic plates collide.
18. _F_ There are relatively few mountain ranges in the world.
19. _T_ Pressure on tectonic plates can cause rocks to fold or bend.
20. _T_ An anticline is formed when rocks bend upward.
21. _F_ A hanging wall is the rock layers below a fault.
22. _T_ A hanging wall moves downward in a normal fault.
23. _F_ Most earthquakes and volcanoes are located around the Atlantic Ocean.
24. _F_ Basaltic volcanoes usually have steep sides.
25. _T_ Scientists cannot accurately predict when a volcano will erupt.

WATER & EROSION

LESSON 27

GEYSERS

HEATED GROUND WATER

SUPPLY LIST

Flexible soda straw   Cup filled with water

BEGINNERS

- What causes a geyser to erupt? **Pressure from water that is heated underground.**

- How is a hot spring different from a geyser? **The water in the pool just bubbles up, but the water in a geyser shoots out.**

- Where can you see many geysers? **Yellowstone National Park.**

WHAT DID WE LEARN?

- What are some ways that heated ground water shows up on the surface of the earth? **Hot springs and pools, spouters, fumaroles, mud pots, mud volcanoes and geysers.**

- Explain how a geyser works. **Underground water is heated and expands inside a network of "plumbing." When the pressure of the heated water becomes greater than the weight of the water above it, it forces water up through the vent.**

- How is a mud pot different from a hot spring? **A mud pot has more dirt than water in it, whereas a spring is mostly just water.**

TAKING IT FURTHER

- How might a scientist figure out which irregular geysers are connected underground? **By observing the behavior of the geysers. If one becomes active at the same time another becomes inactive they might be connected.**

- Why do some hot pools have a rainbow appearance? **The temperature of the water cools as it spreads out and different colored algae and bacteria grow in different temperatures of water.**

- Can you tell the temperature of the water just by looking at a pool? **Maybe. Green colored bacteria begin to grow in water just below 167° F (75° C). Other colors grow in lower temperatures; however, this may not be a completely accurate way to determine temperature.**

CHALLENGE: GEOTHERMAL ENERGY

- Why are geothermal power plants mostly located near edges of tectonic plates? **Because that is where magma is most likely to find its way close to the surface of the earth.**

- Would you expect geothermal power plants to experience more or fewer earthquakes than other power plants? **In general, you would expect more, because they are built in areas that have moving tectonic plates and are more likely to have earthquakes.**

- Why is geothermal energy considered a renewable resource? **The magma and water are not being used up so there is a constant supply of steam. Even though water is "lost" to evaporation, it eventually condenses and returns to the ground through precipitation.**

LESSON 28

WEATHERING & EROSION

IT'S WEARING ME DOWN

SUPPLY LIST

Copy of "Weathering" worksheet   Vinegar   Bar of soap   Soda straw
Real chalk (made from limestone) or a limestone rock   Modeling clay
Supplies for Challenge: Copy of "Chemical Erosion" worksheet   Steel wool (without soap)
3 plastic zipper bags

BEGINNERS

- What is erosion? **When rocks are worn away a little at a time, also called weathering.**

- What happens to a rock when water freezes inside a crack? **The crack gets bigger and eventually the rock will break.**

- What are three ways that rocks can be eroded? **Freezing water, wind, plant roots, chemicals.**

- Does erosion happen slowly or quickly? **Usually it happens slowly, but it can happen quickly during a flood.**

WHAT DID WE LEARN?

- What is weathering? **The wearing down of rocks by natural forces.**

- Describe the two types of weathering. **Chemical—material is changed by chemical reactions; Mechanical—material is worn away by pressure from water/ice, wind, debris, plant roots.**

TAKING IT FURTHER

- How does freezing and thawing of water break rocks? **Water expands when it freezes, breaking off bits of rock and enlarging the crack. After many cycles, the rock will break.**

- What do people do that is similar to mechanical weathering? **People use sand blasting to remove graffiti. Strip mining and dynamite are used to remove rock.**

CHALLENGE: CHEMICAL EROSION WORKSHEET

- Why do you think this sample had the most rust? **Water removes (erodes) the rust from the iron and allows the air in the bag to react with more iron causing more oxidized iron atoms. The bag with water and no air had some rust because of small amounts of oxygen in the air left in the bag and dissolved in the water.**

LESSON 29
MASS WASTING
THE FORCE OF GRAVITY

SUPPLY LIST

Baking tray or large baking pan   Soil and rocks

BEGINNERS

- What force pulls dirt and rocks down a hill? **Gravity.**
- What can trigger a landslide? **Heavy rains or an earthquake.**
- What is an avalanche? **When ice and snow moves quickly down a hill.**

WHAT DID WE LEARN?

- What is mass wasting? **The movement of large amounts of rocks and soil due to gravity.**
- What is slow movement of the soil and rocks down a slope called? **Creep.**
- What is rapid or sudden movement of the soil and rocks called? **A landslide.**

TAKING IT FURTHER

- How does water affect mass wasting? **Water can loosen the bonds between the rocks and soil, allowing gravity to move them more easily.**
- How might weathermen predict when the avalanche danger is high? **The danger might increase when snow suddenly builds up during a storm, when winds are high or when the temperatures begin to warm up. All of these factors can change the strength of the bonds of the snow on the side of the mountain. However, weathermen cannot accurately predict when and where a specific avalanche will occur.**

LESSON 30
STREAM EROSION
THE POWER OF MOVING WATER

SUPPLY LIST

3 baking pans   Soil   Leaves, grass, or other plant material   Book at least 2 inches thick
Supplies for Challenge: Soil   3 paper cups   Pencil   Acces to an oven

BEGINNERS

- What is stream erosion? **Wearing away of rocks and soil by moving water.**
- Why does water flow downhill? **Gravity pulls it down.**
- Does water flow slowly or quickly down a steep hill? **Quickly.**

WHAT DID WE LEARN?

- What is the most powerful eroding force? **Moving water.**

- How does gravity cause stream erosion? **Gravity pulls water downhill. The steeper the hill, the faster and more powerfully the water flows.**

- What is the gradient of a river? **The difference in elevation between the headwaters, or source, and the mouth, or lowest point.**

TAKING IT FURTHER

- Why are farmers concerned about soil erosion? **Topsoil is difficult to replace, so it must be protected to enable the farmers to grow good crops.**

- What are some steps farmers take to prevent water from eroding their topsoil? **They plow crossways to the flow of the water; they alternate crops; they terrace steep areas.**

- Besides water, what other natural force can erode topsoil? **Wind can blow it away.**

- What can farmers do to protect their topsoil from wind erosion? **They can plant trees to block or break up the wind. They can plant shorter rows to keep the wind from blowing soil too far away.**

- Why do lakes and reservoirs have to be dredged, emptied and dug out periodically? **Water from incoming streams deposits silt and rocks in the bottom of the lake and eventually fills it up.**

LESSON 31

SOIL

ISN'T IT JUST DIRT?

SUPPLY LIST

Potting soil   Soil from your yard   Magnifying glass

Supplies for Challenge: Copy of "Permeability of Soil" worksheet   4 paper cups
2–3 cups of soil   Newspaper   Colander   Fine mesh strainer   Stop watch
Liquid measuring cup   Pencils   Baking sheet

BEGINNERS

- What is soil made of? **Bits of sand, clay, silt, and dead plants and animals.**

- Where do bits of sand and clay come from? **They are broken off of rocks by erosion.**

- Is erosion always bad? **No, it helps to make new soil.**

WHAT DID WE LEARN?

- What are the major components of soil? **Sand, silt, clay, organic material (humus).**

- What is the most important element in soil for encouraging plant growth? **Humus—decayed plant matter.**

TAKING IT FURTHER

- What type of rocks would you expect to find near an area with sandy soil? **Quartz rocks.**

- What type of rocks would you expect to find near an area with clay soil? **Feldspar and mica.**

- How does a river that regularly floods, such as the Nile, restore lost topsoil? **Soil is washed into the river by the moving water. When it floods, much of this soil is moved out of the riverbed to the area around the river. As the floodwaters recede, the soil is left behind and can be used for farming.**
- What are some ways that farmers restore nutrients to the soil? **Chemical fertilizers, animal waste, rotating crops, plowing under crops.**

Challenge: Permeability of Soil worksheet

- Which sample had the highest permeability? **Sample 2 should have the highest permeability because it has the largest particles.**
- Which had the lowest permeability? **Sample 4 should have the lowest permeability because it has the smallest particles.**
- How did your unsifted sample (sample 1) compare to the sifted samples? **Sample 1 should be somewhere in between since it is a combination of the other three.**
- How does particle size affect permeability? **The larger the particles the greater the porosity and thus the greater the permeability. In other words, the bigger the particles the more air space there is so the faster the water can flow through.**

LESSON 32

Grand Canyon

Lots of time, little water or lots of water, little time?

Supply list

Modeling clay   Paper   Markers

Beginners

- What are the two main ideas for how Grand Canyon was formed? **A little water over a long time or a lot of water over a little time.**
- Which idea agrees with the Bible? **A lot of water over a little time.**
- Where could a lot of water have come from to make the canyon? **Noah's Flood.**

What did we learn?

- What is the main controversy between evolutionists and creationists concerning the formation of Grand Canyon? **Was it formed by a little water over a long period of time, or by a lot of water over a short period of time?**
- What evidence shows radiometric dating methods to be unreliable? **Rocks at lower levels were dated younger by 100s of millions of years than rocks at higher levels.**

Taking it further

- What event at the eruption of Mount St. Helens supports the biblical view of how Grand Canyon was formed? **A flood resulting from the eruption formed a canyon 100 feet (30 m) wide and 100 feet (30 m) deep through solid rock in only one day. A flood on a much larger scale would have much larger effects.**
- How can scientists look at the exact same data and draw different conclusions? **Everyone has preconceived ideas, or presuppositions, that affect how he or she views the evidence. Evolutionists believe the earth is billions of years old, so they reject any theories that conflict with that idea. Creationists believe what the Bible says and interpret the evidence from that point of view.**

- How can we know what to believe when scientists disagree? **We must trust what God says.**

LESSON 33

CAVES

UNDERGROUND WONDERLANDS

SUPPLY LIST

2 paper or plastic cups   Cotton string   Epsom salt   Cardboard
Supplies for Challenge: Research materials on caves

BEGINNERS

- What is the special name given to the rocks that form when chemicals build up on the ceiling of a cave? **Stalactite.**
- What is the special name given to the rocks that form when chemicals build up on the floor of a cave? **Stalagmite.**
- How are these special rocks formed? **When water passes through limestone it dissolves chemicals that are then left behind in the caves after the water evaporates.**

WHAT DID WE LEARN?

- How are the beautiful formations in caves formed? **Calcite is dissolved in water as it passes through the limestone. As the water evaporates, it leaves the calcite behind, forming beautiful shapes inside the caves.**
- What is a stalactite? **A formation in a cave that hangs from the ceiling.**
- What is a stalagmite? **A formation in a cave that forms on the floor.**

TAKING IT FURTHER

- What evidence do we have that formations in caves can develop rapidly? **Formation has been measured to be rapid in some wet caves. Also, bats and other animals have been found preserved in some stalactites and stalagmites.**
- Why is it likely that calcite formations would have formed rapidly after the Flood? **Conditions would have been very wet inside the caves, with many minerals suspended or dissolved in the water.**
- Besides in caves, where can calcite deposits be found? **Near geysers in places such as Yellowstone National Park.**

QUIZ 4

WATER & EROSION

LESSONS 27–33

Fill in the blank with the correct term from below.

1. A thermal feature that shoots hot water many feet into the air is a **_geyser_**.
2. **_Old Faithful_** is one of the most famous geysers in the world.

3. _Geothermal_ energy can be obtained from areas containing geysers.

4. Geysers often contain _hydrogen sulfide_, which gives them a bad smell.

5. A _fumarole_ is produced when super-heated steam reaches the surface.

6. The process of wearing down rocks is called _weathering_.

7. _Frost heaving_ is the process that brings rocks to the surface each winter.

8. _Mass wasting_ is the effect of gravity pulling soil and rocks down a hill.

9. Rapid movement of large amounts of rocks and soil is called a _landslide_.

10. The most powerful eroding force is _moving water_.

11. The most important component of soil for growing plants is _humus_.

12. _Ash_ can become fertile soil after a volcanic eruption.

13. A formation in a cave that goes from floor to ceiling is called a _column_.

14. _Gravity_ is the force that causes water to move rapidly down a hill.

15. _Limestone_ is the main type of rock from which caves are formed.

CHALLENGE QUESTIONS

Short answer:

16. Where is the most likely place to find geothermal areas? **Near the boundaries of tectonic plates.**

17. List two types of chemical erosion. **Acids, water, oxidation.**

18. Which is more easily eroded, iron or rust? **Rust.**

19. Where are rock glaciers likely to be located? **Steep mountain slopes with cool summers (Colorado and Alaska).**

20. What is a fossil rock glacier? **A rock glacier that no longer has any ice in it.**

21. Which has more power to erode, fast moving water or slow moving water? **Fast moving water.**

22. What is porosity in soil? **The measure of the amount of air space in the soil.**

23. What is permeability of soil? **The speed at which water flows through a sample of soil.**

24. Why are porosity and permeability important? **They affect how well plants will grow in the soil.**

25. What are two indications of a large scale flood found in Grand Canyon? **Two hundred miles of level sedimentary layers, abundant aquatic fossils, nautiloid fossils all lined up the same way, fossilized amphibian and reptile footprints in sandstone.**

26. What is the most interesting thing you learned about caves? **Accept reasonable answers.**

LESSON 34 ROCKS & MINERALS COLLECTION

PUTTING IT ALL TOGETHER

FINAL PROJECT SUPPLY LIST

Rocks and Minerals Guide   Samples of rocks, gems, and minerals   Glue   Markers

Tagboard or poster board   Display box with separated sections (optional)

WHAT DID WE LEARN?

- What are the three types of rocks? **Igneous, sedimentary, and metamorphic.**
- What is a native mineral? **One made from a pure element such as gold or silver.**

TAKING IT FURTHER

- What are some of the greatest or most interesting things you learned from your study of our planet earth? **Accept reasonable answers.**
- Read Genesis chapters 1 and 2. Discuss what was created on each day and how each part completes the whole. **Consider using the drawing lesson at www.answersingenesis.org/docs2002/oh20020301_112. asp to develop this topic.**
- What earth science topic would you like to learn more about? **Have students research at the library or the AiG website and the Internet.**

OUR PLANET EARTH
LESSONS 1–34

Label this diagram of the earth.

A. **Crust**   B. **Mantle**   C. **Outer Core**   D. **Inner Core**

Mark each statement as either True or False.

1. _**T**_ Scientists "see" beneath the crust of the earth using earthquake (seismic) waves.
2. _**F**_ The core is the coolest part of the earth.
3. _**T**_ Magma is liquid rock under the surface of the earth.
4. _**F**_ Coal is not a rock because it is organic.
5. _**F**_ Rocks never change form.
6. _**T**_ Rocks are made from one or more minerals or organic materials.
7. _**T**_ Larger crystals form in igneous rock if it is cooled slowly.
8. _**F**_ All rocks sink in water.
9. _**T**_ Sandstone is a sedimentary rock.
10. _**T**_ Limestone frequently contains fossils.
11. _**F**_ Fossils prove that evolution is true.
12. _**F**_ Fossils prove that creation is true.
13. _**T**_ Natural gas is almost always found near oil deposits.
14. _**F**_ Metamorphic rock can form at low temperatures.
15. _**F**_ Color is the most accurate way to identify a mineral.

Fill in the blank with the correct term from below.

16. The _**1st law of thermodynamics**_ states that matter cannot be created or destroyed.
17. The _**2nd law of thermodynamics**_ states that all systems tend toward a state of chaos.
18. Most _**evolutionists**_ believe that everything in nature happened only by natural processes.
19. _**Uniformitarianism**_ is the belief that everything was formed by the slow processes we observe today.

20. A _**glacier**_ is a thick sheet of ice that does not completely melt each summer.

21. _**Erosional**_ mountains are formed as wind and water erode material away.

22. _**Depositional**_ mountains are formed as layers of sediment are deposited.

23. One of the most dangerous side effects of an earthquake is a _**tsunami**_.

24. When stress due to moving tectonic plates is released it often causes an _**earthquake**_.

25. _**Indonesia**_ is one of the most active volcanic countries in the world.

26. The difference between the base and the peak of a mountain is its _**height**_.

27. The difference between sea level and the peak of a mountain is its _**elevation**_.

Short answer:

28. List two methods used by farmers to reduce soil erosion. **Terracing, crop rotation, plowing across flow of water, wind breaks or ground cover.**

29. The evolutionist view of Grand Canyon is **lots** of time, **little bit** of water.

30. The creationist view of Grand Canyon is **little bit** of time, **lots** of water.

31. Describe the process for the eruption of a geyser. **Water fills underground passages and is heated by magma. When the pressure of the expanded water is greater than the weight of the water above it, the water is forced upward out of the vent.**

32. Explain how water can break a rock. **Water fills a crack then expands as it freezes, making the crack larger. Then the water melts. This process is repeated over and over until the rock breaks. Moving or running water can also wear away at a rock until it breaks.**

CHALLENGE QUESTIONS

Match the term with its definition.

33. _**A**_ Lithification

34. _**E**_ Clasts

35. _**J**_ Matrix

36. _**B**_ Striations

37. _**C**_ Terminal morain

38. _**H**_ Glacial erratic

39. _**D**_ Syncline

40. _**L**_ Foot wall

41. _**F**_ Hanging wall

42. _**G**_ Oxidation

43. _**I**_ Porosity

44. _**K**_ Permeability

LESSON

35

CONCLUSION

THE WONDER OF OUR PLANET EARTH

SUPPLY LIST

Bible   Paper and pencil

OUR WEATHER & WATER

WEATHER & WATER

ATMOSPHERE & METEOROLOGY

A CHRISTIAN VIEW OF WEATHER

WHAT DOES THE BIBLE SAY?

SUPPLY LIST

Copy of "Weather Across the Country" worksheet   Newspaper weather report

Supplies for Challenge: Research materials on various Christian scientists

BEGINNERS

- Who designed the weather patterns on earth? **God did.**

- What is one way that rain and sunshine work together to help people? **They help plants to grow to provide food.**

- What major event in the Bible greatly changed the weather on earth? **The Genesis Flood.**

WHAT DID WE LEARN?

- Is there a Christian view of weather? **Yes, there is a Christian view of everything. Either the weather is only naturalistic, or it is a result of a system designed by God the Creator.**

- What three events described in the Bible have greatly affected the weather on earth? **Creation, the Curse due to the Fall of man, and the Flood.**

- List three things you can learn about the weather from a newspaper weather report. **Actual high and low temperatures, predicted high and low temperatures, precipitation amounts, weather front locations, record high and low temperatures, weather conditions across the country.**

TAKING IT FURTHER

- Why is it important to have a Christian view of weather? **It allows us to recognize God's handiwork.**

- What are some geographical or physical characteristics that affect the weather in a particular area? **Large bodies of water, mountains, deserts, latitude, altitude.**

LESSON 2

STRUCTURE OF THE ATMOSPHERE

LAYERS ABOVE THE EARTH

SUPPLY LIST

Candle   Glass jar   Modeling clay   Matches   Dish
Supplies for Challenge: Graph paper

BEGINNERS

- What is atmosphere? **The gases that surround a planet.**
- What are the two main ingredients in earth's atmosphere? **Nitrogen and oxygen.**
- What are three important things that the atmosphere does? **Provides oxygen to breathe, air pressure for weather, protection from heat and cold, protection from radiation, protection from meteors.**

WHAT DID WE LEARN?

- What are the two main components of air? **Nitrogen—78%, Oxygen—21%.**
- What are the five levels of the atmosphere? **Troposphere, stratosphere, mesosphere, thermosphere, magnetosphere.**
- What are some ways that the atmosphere protects us? **It protects us from extreme temperatures, vacuums, solar radiation and meteors, and provides oxygen to breathe.**

TAKING IT FURTHER

- How would the earth be different if there were a higher concentration of oxygen? **Fires would burn uncontrollably.**
- What would happen if the nitrogen in the atmosphere was replaced with a more reactive element, such as carbon? **The carbon would combine with the oxygen and form carbon dioxide, making the air unbreathable.**

CHALLENGE: ATMOSPHERIC TEMPERATURE

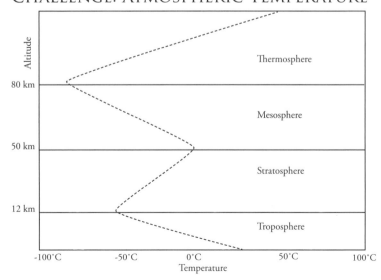

LESSON 3 — THE WEIGHT OF AIR

IT HAS WEIGHT?

SUPPLY LIST

Yard or meter stick   2 identical balloons   Tape   String

Supplies for Challenge: Wide mouth jar   Plastic grocery bag   String or rubberband

BEGINNERS

- Does air have weight? **Yes, a small amount for each molecule.**

- What pulls on the air molecules to make air pressure? **Gravity.**

- Why is air pressure important? **It affects the weather.**

WHAT DID WE LEARN

- What causes air to have weight? **Gravity pulling down on the air molecules.**

- How much air pressure do we experience at sea level? **About 15 pounds per square inch.**

- Why don't we feel the weight of the air molecules? **Our bodies push out with the same amount of pressure.**

- Do you expect air pressure to be the same at all locations in the world? **No, as you go up in altitude, gravity exerts less force on the air molecules so there is less air pressure. Also, the pressure varies from one area to another causing weather fronts.**

TAKING IT FURTHER

- Why is it important that air has weight? **The weight of the air allows us to have wind and moving air fronts.**

- Why must aircraft be pressurized when flying at high altitudes? **The air pressure is much lower at high altitudes than it is on the ground and the lack of pressure can be painful for passengers, especially on their ears as they try to adjust to the lower pressure. If the pressure is low enough, there might not be enough oxygen to breathe.**

LESSON 4 — THE STUDY OF WEATHER

AN INTRODUCTION TO METEOROLOGY

SUPPLY LIST

Lamp   Paper   Scissors   String   Tape

Supplies for Challenge: Copy of "Weather Ingredients" worksheet

BEGINNERS

- What is a meteorologist? **A scientist who studies the weather.**

- What are things that meteorologists measure to help them study the weather? **Temperature, air pressure, wind, and precipitation.**

- Is the air pressure of cold air higher or lower than the air pressure of warm air? **Higher.**

WHAT DID WE LEARN?

- What is meteorology? **The study of the atmosphere; particularly the study of the conditions of the troposphere.**

- What are the five important conditions in the troposphere that meteorologists study? **Temperature, atmospheric/air pressure, humidity, wind, and precipitation.**

TAKING IT FURTHER

- Why are meteorologists interested in studying the conditions of the troposphere? **They want to understand what affects the weather and be able to predict future weather conditions.**

- How does the sun heat areas of the earth that do not receive much direct sunlight? **The sunlight is most concentrated in areas close to the equator. The air is warmer there than at the poles. However, because of air and water currents, warmer air and warmer water move toward the poles and cooler air and water move toward the equator so the earth is more evenly heated.**

CHALLENGE: WEATHER INGREDIENTS WORKSHEET

	Earth	Sun	Air	Water
W	Winter	Waves	Warm/Wind	Wet/White caps
E	Elevation	Eclipse	Expands	Evaporation
A	Absorbs	Angle	Atmosphere	Acid rain
T	Tilted axis	Temperature	Troposphere	Thunderstorm
H	Huge	Heat	Humidity	Hail/Humidity
E	Equator	Energy	Electricity	El Niño/Eye of storm
R	Rotation/Revolution	Radiation/Reflect	Relative humidity	Rain

QUIZ 1

ATMOSPHERE & METEOROLOGY

LESSONS 1–4

Short answer:

1. What does it mean to have a Christian view of weather? **It means to recognize that God designed weather to work the way it does and He controls it. Everything is not just random chance.**

2. Name three things you might find in a local weather report. **Forecasted temperatures and precipitation, actual temperatures and precipitation, location of weather fronts, record temperatures, weather across the country.**

. What is the outermost part of the atmosphere called? **The magnetosphere.**

4. What three events recorded in the Bible drastically affected the surface of the earth? **Creation, Fall, and Flood.**

5. What two gases comprise the majority of our atmosphere? **Nitrogen and oxygen.**

6. List three ways the atmosphere protects life on Earth. **Protects us from the vacuum of space, protects from harmful radiation, protects from extreme temperatures, provides air to breathe.**

7. What are scientists called who study the atmosphere? **meteorologists.**

8. What is temperature? **Measurement of the energy in the atmosphere.**

9. What causes air pressure? **Gravity pulling down on air molecules.**

10. What is absolute humidity? **The total amount of moisture in the air.**

11. What is relative humidity? **The ratio of the amount of moisture in the air to the total amount of moisture the air could hold at the current temperature.**

12. What is precipitation? **Moisture that falls from the atmosphere.**

13. What is the major cause of wind? **Heating of the air by the sun's rays.**

14. Weather occurs in which part of the atmosphere? **Troposphere.**

15. What happens to the atmospheric pressure as you go up in altitude? **The pressure goes down.**

CHALLENGE QUESTIONS

Short answer:

16. Name at least two Christian scientists from the past? **Sir Isaac Newton, Lord Kelvin, Blaise Pascal, Johannes Kepler, Carl Linneaus, Robert Boyle, Charles Babbage, Joseph Lister, Georges Cuvier, David Brewster, Louis Pasteur, James Clerk Maxwell.**

17. What is lapse rate with respect to the atmosphere? **The rate at which the temperature decreases as you increase in altitude.**

18. Name two gases that are lighter than air. **Hydrogen and helium.**

19. Briefly explain how each of the following contributes to weather formation.

    Sun: **Generates energy waves that heat up the earth.**

    Earth: **Absorbs heat from the sun and radiates it into the atmosphere.**

    Air: **Absorbs heat from the sun and the earth causing molecules to move around and changes air pressure creating wind and weather fronts.**

    Water: **Evaporation and condensation of water contributes to much of the weather we experience.**

20. Does temperature always decrease with altitude? Explain your answer. **No. Above the troposphere temperatures increase with altitude through the stratosphere, decrease with altitutde in the mesosphere, and increase with altitutde in the thermosphere.**

UNIT 2
ANCIENT WEATHER & CLIMATE

LESSON 5

WEATHER VS. CLIMATE

WHAT'S THE DIFFERENCE?

SUPPLY LIST

Copy of "Weather vs. Climate" worksheet   Newspaper weather report   World atlas

Supplies for Challenge: Copy of world map   Colored pencils   World atlas

BEGINNERS

- What is weather? **The conditions outside at a particular time.**

- What is climate? **The weather over a long period of time—average weather.**

- Name at least three different kinds of climate. **Polar, desert, tropical, sub-tropical, temperate, etc.**

WHAT DID WE LEARN?

- What is weather? **The atmospheric conditions present in an area at a given time.**

- What is climate? **The average weather conditions for an area over a long period of time, including average temperatures and average precipitation.**

- What are the five major climates found on earth? **Polar, desert, tropical, subtropical, and temperate.**

TAKING IT FURTHER

- How does the Gobi Desert help create the monsoon? **The Gobi Desert heats the dry air around it. That air rises, allowing cooler air to move in. The cooler air comes from the Bay of Bengal and has a high moisture content, thus bringing rain to the area near the bay.**

- Which of the following phrases describe weather and which describe climate?

  Cloudy with a chance of rain: **Weather.**

  Average of 20 inches of rain per year: **Climate.**

  Average summer temperature of 70°F: **Climate.**

  3 inches of snow in the past 24 hours: **Weather.**

WEATHER & WATER

LESSON 6

PRE-FLOOD CLIMATE

WAS IT DIFFERENT?

SUPPLY LIST

Mirror   House plant   Plate or shallow dish

Supplies for Challenge: Copy of "Climate Clues" worksheet

BEGINNERS

- What clues does the Bible give about what the climate was like before the Flood? **That it was likely warm worldwide; Adam and Eve were comfortable without clothes.**

- What clues do fossils give us about what the climate was like before the Flood? **There were tropical plants in nearly every part of the world, so it was probably warmer around the world.**

WHAT DID WE LEARN?

- Using clues from the Bible and science, what was the climate most likely like on earth before the Flood? **Warm, possibly no rain and more water vapor in the atmosphere, more constant temperature.**

TAKING IT FURTHER

- How does the Bible say that plants were watered in the beginning? **The Bible says they were watered by springs and rivers. They were also probably watered by dew and from underground sources.**

- How might the breaking up of the original landmass have contributed to the Flood? **Superheated water from inside the earth would have shot into the atmosphere and then rained back to earth.**

CHALLENGE: CLIMATE CLUES WORKSHEET

Clue #1:

1. Where do swamp cypress trees grow today? **Swampy areas in Georgia and Florida.**

2. What is the climate like in the Arctic Islands today? **Very cold and snowy.**

3. What possible explanation could there be for how the cypress tree fossils were formed in the Arctic Islands? **It may have been much warmer and wetter in the past so the trees could grow there, or the cypress trees were carried there from another location and then fossilized.**

Clue #2:

1. Where do hippopotami live today? **In grasslands where there is still water or in forests in Africa.**

2. What kind of plant life is required to support elephants? **An elephant eats 200–400 pounds of grass and other plants each day.**

3. Do many people live in villages in the Sahara Desert today? **Although there are some villages, most people that live in the desert are nomads.**

4. What can you conclude about the climate in the Sahara area before the Flood? **There must have been a lot more water and grass to support the life that was there.**

Clue #3:

1. What is the climate like in Antarctica today? **It is very cold and snowy—mostly frozen.**

2. What kind of plant life is required to support dinosaurs? **It depends what kind of dinosaurs they were; they either ate plants or they ate the animals that ate the plants.**

3. What kind of plant life exists in Antarctica today? **There is very little plant life there.**

4. What can you conclude about the climate in Antarctica before the Flood? **It was probably much warmer than it is now.**

CLIMATE CHANGES DUE TO THE GENESIS FLOOD

GOD'S PUNISHMENT FOR SIN

SUPPLY LIST

Paper   Drawing materials (colored pencils, markers, etc.)

BEGINNERS

- What was the weather like after the Genesis Flood? **The temperatures were cooler and there was more snow.**
- Was the whole world covered with ice during the Ice Age? **No, areas near the equator still had very pleasant weather.**
- What happened to all the ice from the Ice Age? **Much of it melted and went into the oceans. Some of it is still ice at the North and South Poles.**

WHAT DID WE LEARN?

- What was the earth's climate like before the Flood? **Probably more uniformly warm and tropical.**
- What was the climate like after the Flood? **It was much cooler and wetter than today. Ice covered much of the earth. It was still temperate in the areas near the equator.**
- Approximately how much of the world was covered with ice during the Ice Age? **30%.**
- What two weather conditions are necessary for an ice age to form? **Cool summers and wet/snowy winters.**

TAKING IT FURTHER

- Why did God send a huge Flood? **To destroy man because of his wickedness.**
- What evidence points to a warmer pre-Flood climate? **Fossils of tropical plants around the world.**
- What evidence points to an ice age? **Valleys cut by glaciers, frozen plants and animals, fossils in ice, etc.**
- Do we see new glaciers forming today? **Yes, we see some new glaciers forming and some old glaciers growing bigger for a few years, but not on the large scale that occurred during the Ice Age.**

LESSON 8

GLOBAL WARMING

FACT OR FICTION

SUPPLY LIST

Newspaper articles about global warming

BEGINNERS

- What is global warming? **The belief that the earth is warming up due to pollution and other factors.**
- Have scientists proven that global warming is a problem? **No, there is a small increase in temperature, but we don't know if that is really a problem or not.**
- What traps more heat near the earth than carbon dioxide? **Water vapor and clouds in the air.**

WHAT DID WE LEARN?

- What is global warming? **The increase in average temperature around the earth.**
- What is the greenhouse effect? **Heat is trapped in the atmosphere and not released back into space.**
- What is the main cause of the greenhouse effect? **Water vapor in the atmosphere.**
- What amount of greenhouse effect is due to carbon dioxide in the atmosphere? **Only about 5%.**
- How much has the temperature increased over the past 130 years? **Only about 1.2°F.**
- Name at least two possible natural causes for increased temperatures. **Increased energy from the sun, decreased volcanic activity, increased cloud cover.**

TAKING IT FURTHER

- Why is it important to know what assumptions are made when looking at computer models? **The assumptions greatly affect the outcome. If bad assumptions are made, then the results are unreliable.**
- Ice core samples from Greenland indicate that rapid climate shifts have occurred in the past. How can your worldview affect the interpretation of this data? **If you believe the Bible you would expect to see rapid climate changes due to the Flood and its aftermath. If you believe in evolutionary processes and slow changes, this data can be very alarming and cause people to look for possible rapid climate changes in the future.**

QUIZ 2

ANCIENT WEATHER & CLIMATE

LESSONS 5–8

Match the term with its definition.

1. _F_ Conditions in the atmosphere at a given time
2. _C_ Average weather conditions over a long time
3. _I_ Very dry climate
4. _A_ Wet warm climate year round

5. _H_ How plants were watered in the beginning

6. _B_ Event believed to be triggered by the Flood

7. _D_ Trapping of heat in the earth's atmosphere

8. _E_ Increase in earth's average temperature due to increased carbon dioxide

9. _J_ Climate with four distinct seasons

10. _G_ Climate with cooler winters than topical areas

Mark each statement as either True or False.

11. _T_ Average global temperatures have increased in the past 150 years.

12. _F_ Carbon dioxide is the main cause of the greenhouse effect.

13. _F_ It has been proven that global warming is caused by man's actions.

14. _T_ The earth's climate was probably more uniformly tropical before the Flood.

15. _F_ The Flood did not change the earth very much.

16. _T_ The Bible indicates there may have been one landmass before the Flood.

17. _F_ The climate changes from day to day.

18. _T_ Deserts can be cold.

19. _T_ The monsoon brings rain to much of Southeast Asia.

20. _F_ We should just ignore global warming.

CHALLENGE QUESTIONS

Short answer:

21. Describe the Coriolis effect. **Circular air currents develop due to the rotation of the earth—primarily counter clockwise in the northern hemisphere and clockwise in the southern hemisphere.**

22. In an area that primarily experiences updrafts would you expect the weather to be wet or dry? Why would you expect this? **Rising air increases precipitation so it would be wet.**

23. Explain how finding fossils of dinosaurs in Antarctica gives a clue to its past climate. **In order for dinosaurs to exist they need plants or other animals to eat, so the climate had to have been warm enough to support this kind of life.**

24. How could the climate in an area have changed quickly in the past? **The Genesis Flood caused many changes to the earth, which greatly affected the climate in a short period of time. In general rapid climate changes do not occur; the Flood was a very unusual event.**

25. Give an example of how global warming could be a beneficial thing. **Longer growing seasons, increased precipitation, fewer deaths due to the cold, increased shipping in northern areas.**

LESSON 9

WATER CYCLE

THE ULTIMATE IN RECYCLING

SUPPLY LIST

Paper   Colored pencils

BEGINNERS

- What process has God provided as a way for water to be used over and over again? **The water cycle.**
- How does water get moved out of the oceans? **It is heated by the sun and turns to a gas—evaporation.**
- How does water get back to land? **The wind moves the wet air over the land; when the air cools, the water leaves the air as rain or snow—precipitation.**

WHAT DID WE LEARN?

- How does water vapor enter the atmosphere? **Through evaporation, transpiration, and vaporization.**
- Which of these processes accounts for most of the water in the air? **Evaporation.**
- How does water get from the atmosphere back to the earth? **Through precipitation such as rain, snow, sleet, dew, and hail.**

TAKING IT FURTHER

- What are some factors that affect how fast the water evaporates from the surface of the ocean or lake? **Wind, heat, and the dryness of the air all affect the rate of evaporation.**
- Why is it better to water your grass early in the morning rather than later in the day during the summer? **The air is hotter in the middle of the day and more of the water will evaporate and less will soak into the ground to help the grass grow.**

LESSON 10

CLOUD FORMATION

PRETTY WHITE SHAPES IN THE SKY

SUPPLY LIST

Pan of water   Jar with a lid   Plastic zipper bag   Ice

Supplies for Challenge: 2 shoe boxes (one must be smaller than the other)   Gloves
Lid or cardboard for smaller shoe box   Several small pieces of dry ice   Newspaper   Towel
Black construction paper   Hammer   Flashlight

BEGINNERS

- What is a cloud? **A bunch of water drops together in the sky.**

- How does the water get into the air? **The sun heats surface water causing water to turn into gas, which goes into the air.**

- Why does the water gas turn into liquid water? **The air cools down and the water turns back into liquid.**

- Why do clouds float? **Rising air pushes up on the water drops, keeping them suspended in the air.**

WHAT DID WE LEARN?

- What is a cloud? **A mass of water droplets or ice crystals suspended in the air.**

- What is the dew point of air? **The point at which the air is holding the maximum amount of water for the current temperature.**

- What is another name for dew point? **100% relative humidity.**

- How do clouds form? **Warm moist air rises. As it rises, it cools. Eventually it reaches the dew point and water condenses on dust and pollen particles to form clouds.**

TAKING IT FURTHER

- Often, one side of a mountain range receives much more rain than the other side. Why do you think this happens? **If the winds come primarily from one direction, clouds will form more often on the near side of the mountain. As these clouds are forced to rise, they cool and can no longer hold all of the water, resulting in precipitation on that side of the mountain.**

- Why don't clouds always result in rain? **If the air around a cloud is dry, the water in the cloud will evaporate again instead of raining.**

- What role do pollen and dust play in cloud formation? **Water at dew point needs something on which to condense. Dust and pollen particles in the air provide this and thus encourage condensation and cloud formation.**

LESSON
11

CLOUD TYPES

A BEAUTIFUL VARIETY

SUPPLY LIST

Blue construction paper   Glue   Cotton balls
Supplies for Challenge: Clear 2-liter plastic bottle   Match   Warm water

BEGINNERS

- What are flat sheets of clouds called? **Stratus clouds.**

- What are fluffy clouds called? **Cumulus clouds.**

- What are wispy or curly clouds called? **Cirrus clouds.**

What did we learn?

- What are the two ways that clouds are classified? **By shape and altitude.**
- What are the three main shapes of clouds and how does each look? **Stratus—stretched out layers; cumulus—heaped, piled up, and fluffy; cirrus—curly or wispy.**
- What are rain clouds called? **Nimbus clouds.**

Taking it further

- What would a fluffy cloud at 0.5 miles (0.8 km) be called? **Stratocumulus.**
- What would a wispy cloud at 5 miles (8 km) above the earth be called? **Cirrus—it would be cirrus by shape and cirrus by altitude but would not be called cirrocirrus, just cirrus.**

LESSON

12 Precipitation

Rain, rain go away

Supply list

Flour   Pie pan/baking dish   Rain/water   Access to oven

Supplies for Challenge: pH testing paper (optional)   Samples of water from various locations near your home

Beginners

- What is precipitation? **Water coming out of the air.**
- Name three types of precipitation. **Rain, snow, hail.**
- How do raindrops form? **Tiny drops of water in a cloud stick together to form bigger drops that become rain.**

What did we learn?

- What are the main types of precipitation? **Dew, frost, drizzle, rain, sleet, hail, and snow.**
- What is the difference between drizzle and rain? **Drizzle is very tiny drops; rain is water droplets larger than 0.02 inches (0.05 cm).**
- What shape do snowflakes have? **Each is unique but they all have six sides—hexagonal.**
- What is coalescence? **When water droplets begin to stick together to form bigger drops.**
- What is the difference between sleet and hail? **Sleet is very small ice pellets, while hail is larger pellets of ice.**

Taking it further

- What conditions are necessary for large hailstones to form? **Warm humid conditions are needed to form the strong updrafts necessary to keep the ice pellets in the air long enough to become hail.**
- How effective is cloud seeding? **No one really knows. Only clouds that are likely to produce rain are seeded, so it is impossible to tell if the rain was caused naturally or as a result of the seeding.**

QUIZ 3

CLOUDS

LESSONS 9–12

Fill in the blank with the correct term from below.

1. Water vapor enters the atmosphere primarily through _evaporation_.

2. The _water cycle_ describes how water is reused over and over.

3. _Precipitation_ is water that is leaving the atmosphere.

4. When water vapor condenses in the atmosphere it forms a _cloud_.

5. A bubble of warm moist air is called a _convection cell_.

6. _Stratus_ clouds form in layers or sheets.

7. Big fluffy clouds are called _cumulus_ clouds.

8. _Cirrus_ clouds are wispy and curly.

9. Clouds that are likely to produce rain are called _nimbus_ clouds.

10. _Hail_ is large frozen pellets of ice falling from the atmosphere.

11. Water that crystallizes in the clouds and falls to the earth is called _snow_.

12. A long period without precipitation is called a _drought_.

13. _Drizzle_ is tiny droplets of water too small to be called rain.

14. All snowflakes have _six_ sides.

15. _Cloud seeding_ is sometimes used to try to produce rain.

16. Only about _ten_ percent of all clouds produce precipitation.

CHALLENGE QUESTIONS

Mark each statement as either True or False.

17. _F_ The water table is the surface of a lake.

18. _T_ Water flows through permeable rock.

19. _T_ Fog is a cloud that touches the ground.

20. _F_ Radiation fog occurs on windy nights.

21. _T_ Coastal areas often experience advection fog.

22. _T_ Water droplets require a condensation nucleus to coalesce.

23. _T_ Upslope fog occurs near mountains.

24. _F_ Acid rain is a myth.

25. _T_ Rain water is naturally acidic.

WEATHER & WATER

STORMS

LESSON 13

AIR MASSES & WEATHER FRONTS

CREATING THE WEATHER

SUPPLY LIST

Empty 2-liter plastic bottle

BEGINNERS

- What do scientists call a large amount of air that is all the same temperature and humidity? **Air mass.**
- What is a weather front? **Where two air masses meet and the air gets all jumbled.**
- What things often occur at a weather front? **Clouds form, precipitation, and wind.**

WHAT DID WE LEARN?

- What is an air mass? **A large amount of air that has uniform temperature and humidity.**
- How do air masses form? **When there is very little wind in an area, the air does not move around much and becomes uniform.**
- How does the air pressure compare between warm and cold air masses? **Warm air masses usually have lower air pressure than cold air masses.**

TAKING IT FURTHER

- How would a cold air mass that develops over land be classified? **A continental polar air mass.**
- Why do most weather changes occur along weather fronts? **Air becomes very unsettled along a front. This allows air to heat up and cool down, which encourages precipitation. The air pressure, temperature, and humidity levels are different from one air mass to another, so when one air mass displaces another it will probably change the weather.**

LESSON 14

WIND

HOLD ONTO YOUR HAT

SUPPLY LIST

Metal clothes hanger   Large trash bag   Masking tape

BEGINNERS

- What is wind? **Moving air.**

- Does wind move from cold areas to warm areas or from warm areas to cold areas? **From cold to warm.**

- What ultimately causes the wind to blow? **Heat from the sun.**

- Why is wind important? **It moves the weather fronts that bring precipitation.**

WHAT DID WE LEARN?

- What is the main cause of wind? **The sun heats the earth and air. Hot air rises and cooler air moves in to take its place.**

- What is a jet stream? **A very fast moving current of air high in the atmosphere.**

- What are trade winds? **Winds that consistently blow in a particular direction in an area of the ocean during a particular season.**

TAKING IT FURTHER

- Why was it important for sailors of sailing ships to know about trade winds, doldrums, and other prevailing winds? **They could use the winds to help them sail faster, and they wanted to avoid the doldrums. Today's ships are not dependent on wind so this is not as big of an issue for shipping today as it used to be.**

- Why does the breeze near the coast blow toward the land in the morning and toward the sea at night? **Land heats and cools faster than water so the air above the land heats faster than the air above the water during the day and cools faster after sunset.**

LESSON 15

THUNDERSTORMS

LIGHTNING AND THUNDER

WEATHER & WATER

SUPPLY LIST

Furry stuffed animal   Piece of cloth

BEGINNERS

- When do thunderstorms usually happen in temperate areas? **In the summer.**

- Where do most thunderstorms occur? **Near the equator.**

- Where should you be during a thunderstorm? **Inside a building.**

WHAT DID WE LEARN?

- What is a thunderstorm? **A large storm with high winds, lots of rain, thunder, and lightning.**

- What causes lightning? **Water particles and ice crystals rub against each other creating ions. Positive ions collect at the top of the cloud and negative ions collect at the bottom. When these ions connect, energy is released in the form of light.**

- What causes thunder? **Lightning heats the air, causing it to expand and then contract very quickly as it cools, which causes an explosive sound.**

TAKING IT FURTHER

- Why does hail form in thunderstorms that have high clouds? **Higher clouds form when the air is moving more quickly up and down. At higher altitudes the water freezes, forming ice pellets and the faster moving air forces the pellets up into the cloud over and over, forming hail.**

- Why do thunderstorms usually form on hot summer days? **The hotter the air, the more it will expand causing more updrafts and bigger clouds.**

CHALLENGE: FLASH FLOODS

- **Things you can do to be safe in a severe thunderstorm include: Monitor the weather station when severe storms are likely so you have as much warning as possible. Seek shelter inside a house or other building. Stay away from water. Because of the electrical nature of lightning, avoid using the telephone or taking a shower during a severe storm and do not touch metal pipes, fences, or wires. Do not stand on a hilltop; avoid being the tallest object around if you are stuck outside. Get to higher ground if a flash flood is predicted.**

LESSON 16

TORNADOES

SWIRLING WIND

SUPPLY LIST

Two empty 2-liter plastic bottles   Duct tape
Plastic tornado tube connector (optional but recommended)

BEGINNERS

- What is a tornado? **A giant swirling cloud.**
- Where do most tornadoes happen? **In the eastern ⅔ of the U.S.**
- Where is the safest place to be during a tornado? **In a basement under a set of stairs.**

WHAT DID WE LEARN?

- What causes a tornado to develop? **Warm updrafts suck cool downdrafts into them. The falling drier air can cause the updraft to begin to spiral. If there is enough heat and energy, the spiral can tighten and speed up, resulting in a tornado.**
- What is the difference between a funnel cloud and a tornado? **A funnel cloud does not touch the ground.**
- What is a waterspout? **A tornado that develops over the water.**
- When do most tornadoes occur in the United States? **In the springtime.**

TAKING IT FURTHER

- How does the jet stream affect tornado formation? **The jet stream is a fast moving current of air at high altitudes. It can cause the air in a thunderstorm to move more quickly, adding energy to the storm. This encourages tornado formation.**
- Why should you take shelter during a tornado? **The greatest threat to people during a tornado is flying debris. Taking shelter can protect you from the debris.**

LESSON 17

HURRICANES

TYPHOONS

SUPPLY LIST

Copy of "Storm Word Scramble"

BEGINNERS

- What are the largest storms in the world called? **Hurricanes.**
- Where do hurricanes form? **Over the ocean where it is warm, near the equator.**
- What are two reasons that a hurricane causes damage when it reaches land? **It has high winds; tornadoes can form at its edges; storm surge causes flooding.**

STORM WORD SCRAMBLE

1. When warm, moist air cools. **condensation**
2. A large amount of air with uniform temperature and humidity. **air mass**
3. Where two air masses meet. **front**
4. Air movements caused by the sun heating the ground more near the equator than at the poles. **global winds**
5. A very high, fast-moving current of air. **jet stream**
6. Phenomenon caused when ions discharge energy in a cloud. **lightning**
7. A spiraling cloud that does not touch the ground. **funnel cloud**
8. A tornado that forms over water. **waterspout**
9. A hurricane that forms in the Pacific Ocean. **typhoon**
10. Rising sea level in front of a hurricane. **storm surge**
11. Equipment used by National Weather Service to predict tornadoes and hurricanes. **Doppler radar**
12. Person who studies the weather. **meteorologist**
13. Location where 90% of hurricanes form. **Pacific Ocean**
14. Type of cloud found in thunderstorms. **cumulonimbus**
15. Instrument for indicating wind direction. **wind sock**

WHAT DID WE LEARN?

- What is a hurricane? **A huge storm that develops over warm waters.**
- Where do most hurricanes occur? **In the western Pacific Ocean.**
- What is the difference between a tropical depression, a tropical storm, and a hurricane? **Tropical depression has wind speeds of 25–38 mph; tropical storm has wind speeds of 39–73 mph; and a hurricane has wind speeds of at least 74 mph.**

TAKING IT FURTHER

- Why does a hurricane dissipate once it reaches land? **The storm is fueled or energized by the warm moist air of the tropical ocean. Once it reaches land, the energy to keep the storm going is no longer there.**

- How does warm water help create and energize a hurricane? **The warm water easily evaporates and the warm air rises. As it rises, the air cools and the water condenses. The condensing water releases heat causing more water to evaporate setting up a cycle that can result in hurricane formation.**

QUIZ 4

STORMS

LESSONS 13–17

Choose the best answer for each question or statement.

1. _B_ Most weather is determined by the location and movement of _____.
2. _A_ When two air masses meet what do they form?
3. _D_ An air mass has uniform _____.
4. _C_ Which weather phenomenon keeps temperatures more even on the earth?
5. _A_ When the wind blows from the sea to the land it is called a _____.
6. _A_ Winds that blow straight up consistently are called _____.
7. _C_ About the highest altitude that thunderstorms can reach is _____.
8. _A_ God provides a way to return nitrogen to the soil through _____.
9. _D_ A spiraling cloud that does not touch the ground is called a _____.
10. _A_ Hurricanes lose power when they _____.
11. _C_ A tropical cyclone that begins in the Northwest Pacific Ocean is called a _____.
12. _A_ The explosive sound caused by expanding and contracting air in a thunderstorm is _____.

CHALLENGE QUESTIONS

Fill in the blank with the correct term from below.

13. A warm front generally moves from _west_ to _east_.
14. A _cold_ front generally moves more quickly than a _warm_ front.
15. Jet streams are stronger during the _winter_ than in the _summer_.
16. Jet streams play a role in the formation of _tornadoes_.
17. You should climb to higher ground in the event of a _flash flood_.
18. _Doppler_ radar is used to determine the speed and direction that a storm is moving.
19. _Phased array_ radar will be able to scan the atmosphere much more quickly than current radar.
20. _Hurricane Hunters_ fly their airplanes through hurricanes and other storms.
21. Weather satellites allow scientists to view all of a _hurricane_ at one time.
22. _TOTO_ was a portable weather station placed in the path of a tornado.
23. A _dropsonde_ is a portable weather station dropped into a hurricane.
24. Because of the jet stream it is often faster to fly from _west_ to _east_.

WEATHER INFORMATION

GATHERING WEATHER INFORMATION

WHAT IS THE WEATHER LIKE?

SUPPLY LIST

2 thermometers   Rubber band   Cotton cloth   Dish of water   Sling psychrometer (optional)

BEGINNERS

- What does a thermometer measure? **Temperature.**
- What does a barometer measure? **Air pressure.**
- What does a psychrometer measure? **Relative humidity—water in the air.**

WHAT DID WE LEARN?

- What does a meteorologist measure with a thermometer? **Temperature of the air.**
- What is air temperature? **A measure of the movement of air molecules indicating the energy they possess.**
- What are the two temperature scales commonly used? **Fahrenheit and Celsius.**
- What does a meteorologist measure with a barometer? **Air pressure.**
- What is air pressure? **The amount of pressure or force that the air exerts on the earth.**
- What does a meteorologist measure with a psychrometer? **Relative humidity.**
- What is relative humidity? **The ratio of the amount of moisture in the air to the amount of moisture the air could hold at the current temperature.**

TAKING IT FURTHER

- Why does a sling psychrometer give faster results than a stationary psychrometer? **The wet bulb of a sling psychrometer is exposed to dry air more quickly because of its movement, so water evaporates more quickly, giving a faster reading.**
- Why do thermometers need to be kept out of direct sunlight? **The energy from the sun will directly heat the liquid in the thermometer and will give a higher reading than the air temperature around it.**

LESSON 19

MORE WEATHER INSTRUMENTS

WHAT ELSE DO THEY USE?

SUPPLY LIST

Jar with flat bottom   Ruler   Tape   Waterproof marker

BEGINNERS

- What does a weather vane, or wind sock, measure? **Wind direction.**
- What does an anemometer measure? **Wind speed.**
- What does a rain gauge measure? **Rainfall.**
- How do scientists take measurements of the weather up in the atmosphere? **They send instruments up into the air with giant balloons.**

WHAT DID WE LEARN?

- How do meteorologists measure wind? **An anemometer measures wind speed and a wind sock or wind vane indicates wind direction.**
- How do meteorologists measure weather at higher altitudes? **With weather balloons carrying radio-sondes—boxes with weather instruments that transmit measurements back to the weather station.**
- What sophisticated instruments do meteorologists use? **Radar, Doppler radar, satellites, and computers.**

TAKING IT FURTHER

- Why is it important for a meteorologist to take weather readings at higher altitudes? **This gives him/her a picture of the entire weather system. It shows the size of air masses and it shows where weather fronts are occurring.**
- Why might a weather satellite be useful for tracking a hurricane? **A satellite can show the whole storm as well as its path in relation to landmasses.**
- Why are computers necessary for weather tracking and forecasting? **The amount of data needed to understand the weather is enormous. Computers can take all of that data and analyze it and print it in formats that are easier for people to read and understand.**

LESSON 20

REPORTING & ANALYZING WEATHER INFORMATION

MAKING IT ALL MAKE SENSE

SUPPLY LIST

Copy of "Weather Station Model" worksheet

BEGINNERS

- Where are weather instruments located? **All over the earth: on land, on ships, on airplanes, and on satellites.**

- What happens to the information from all these weather instruments? **It is sent to a computer that uses it to generate many different maps**.

WEATHER STATION MODEL WORKSHEET

1. How much of the sky is covered with clouds? **Complete cloud cover (100%).**
2. From which direction is the wind blowing? **Southwest.**
3. What is the wind speed? **15 knots.**
4. What is the current temperature? **78°F.**
5. Is any precipitation falling? If so, what kind? **Yes, rain.**
6. What is the current dew point? **40°F.**
7. What is the current air pressure? **1015.8 millibars .**

WHAT DID WE LEARN?

- What happens to the weather data collected at weather stations? **The information is sent to the National Weather Service where it is compiled and analyzed, and then used to generate weather charts and maps, and to make forecasts.**

- Other than from land-based weather stations, where does the National Weather Service get weather information? **From airborne radiosondes, aircrafts, ships, radar, and satellites.**

- What does the Surface Weather Map show? **The low pressure areas, precipitation, and weather fronts on the surface of the earth.**

TAKING IT FURTHER

- Why is it necessary for one location to collect and analyze all of the weather data across the United States? **Air masses change the weather as they move across the country. It is necessary to know where the different air masses are, how big they are, and in what directions they are moving. This can only be obtained by compiling measurements from multiple locations.**

- Why is a standard picture type or model needed for reporting weather information? **God designed people to be able to quickly process pictures into information, so anyone looking at the model can immediately see the weather conditions in a particular area. This is faster and easier than a written description.**

- Why must the information in the model be converted to electrical signals before it is transmitted to the National Weather Service's computer? **Computers only deal with electrical signals; pictures are for humans.**

LESSON
21

FORECASTING THE WEATHER

MAKING PREDICTIONS

SUPPLY LIST

Copy of "Weather Forecasting" worksheet   Newspaper weather report

Supplies for Challenge: Graph paper   Colored pencils

BEGINNERS

- Who makes the weather forecasts that we see on TV and in the newspaper? **Local weather people.**

- Where do local weather people get the information to make weather forecasts? **From the maps generated by the computers at the National Weather Service.**

- Are weather forecasts always right? **No, sometimes the weather does something unexpected.**

- Who is ultimately in charge of the weather? **God.**

WHAT DID WE LEARN?

- How do meteorologists predict what the weather will be like? **Weather data from around the country and around the world is fed into a computer that generates weather forecasts for each area of the country. Local meteorologists use these forecasts as well as their own experience to predict what the weather will be like for the next several days.**

- What is an important function of local National Weather Service offices? **They monitor weather conditions and put out warnings and alerts when dangerous weather conditions are likely to develop.**

TAKING IT FURTHER

- Why are weather forecasts more accurate today than they were 20 years ago? **New computer programs are able to compile more information and make better models of the weather, plus more information is available.**

- Are weather forecasts always reliable? **No, the weather is very complicated and will never be fully understood. God is the only one who knows exactly what the weather will be.**

LESSON

22 WEATHER STATION

COLLECTING YOUR OWN DATA

FINAL PROJECT SUPPLY LIST

Copy of "Weather Data Sheet"   Clear plastic tubing   Food coloring   Modeling clay
Waterproof marker   String   Empty bottle   6-inch ruler   Soda straw   Duct tape
Thin stick or skewer   Cardboard or tagboard   Weather station with an anemometer (optional)

WHAT DID WE LEARN?

- What does each instrument in your weather station measure? **Thermometer—temperature; psychrometer—relative humidity; wind sock—wind direction; anemometer—wind speed; barometer—air pressure; rain gauge—precipitation.**

TAKING IT FURTHER

- Why might you want to have your own weather station? **It's fun and educational.**

- Why might your weather readings be different from what is reported in the newspaper or on TV? **Your instruments are not as accurate and they are taking their measurements in a different location.**

- Did you see any relationship between air pressure and wind and rain? **You most likely noticed that when the air pressure changed there was more wind. Also, lower air pressure indicates a warm front that usually has more moisture and is more likely to bring rain. Higher air pressure usually indicates a cold front that is likely to have drier air and is less likely to bring rain.**

- What changes did you see in your temperature readings from day to day? **Answers will vary.**

QUIZ 5

WEATHER INFORMATION

LESSONS 18–22

Mark each statement as either True or False.

1. _T_ A meteorologist is someone who studies the weather.
2. _F_ A barometer is used to measure temperature.
3. _F_ Air pressure goes up as you go up in altitude.
4. _T_ A psychrometer is used to measure relative humidity in the air.
5. _F_ All weather sayings are superstitious myths.
6. _T_ Meteorologists use many different instruments to understand the weather.
7. _T_ Wind direction can be shown by using a wind sock.
8. _T_ Weather satellites are very valuable tools for meteorologists.
9. _F_ Weather balloons are used to measure the weather on the ground.
10. _T_ Doppler radar can help detect severe storms more quickly than regular radar.
11. _T_ Computers are very important tools for meteorologists.
12. _F_ A weather station model is not useful for conveying information.
13. _T_ The National Weather Service helps local meteorologists make forecasts.
14. _F_ Weather forecasts were more accurate before computers were used.
15. _T_ You can collect weather data at home.
16. _F_ An anemometer shows wind direction.
17. _F_ With enough information anyone can predict the weather accurately.
18. _T_ Aircrafts and ships are used to help collect weather data.
19. _T_ A rain gauge collects rain to show how much precipitation has fallen.
20. _T_ God ultimately controls the weather.

CHALLENGE QUESTIONS

Match the term with its definition.

_C_ 21. Equivalent temperature if the air was dry and still
_B_ 22. Calculation using temperature and relative humidity
_D_ 23. Calculation using temperature and wind speed
_E_ 24. Satellite stays over the same earth location
_A_ 25. Satellite moves over the earth's poles

Short answer:

26. Pete is outside when the temperature is 40°F and the wind is blowing at 15 miles per hour. Polly is outside when the temperature is 30°F and the wind is blowing at 5 miles per hour. Who is likely to feel more comfortable? **Polly; Pete's apparent temp. is 22.4°F; Polly's apparent temp. is 26.9°F.**

27. Paul is outside when the temperature is 90°F and the relative humidity is 50%. Patty is outside when the temperature is 85°F and the relative humidity is 80%. Who is likely to feel more comfortable? **Paul; Paul's apparent temp. is 94.6°F; Patty's apparent temp. is 96.8°F.**

UNIT 6
OCEAN MOVEMENT

LESSON 23

OVERVIEW OF THE OCEANS
EXPLORING THE SEAS

SUPPLY LIST

Copy of world map   World atlas   Colored pencils or markers

BEGINNERS

- What are the names of the five oceans? **Pacific, Atlantic, Indian, Antarctic, and Arctic.**
- Which ocean is the largest ocean? **Pacific.**
- In which ocean are most of the fish caught that people eat? **Atlantic.**
- Why are oceans important to weather? **Most rain and snow comes from water that has evaporated over the oceans; many storms form over the oceans then move to land; oceans keep the water cycle going.**

WHAT DID WE LEARN?

- What are the names of the five oceans? **Pacific, Atlantic, Indian, Antarctic (or Southern), and Arctic.**
- Which ocean is the largest? **The Pacific Ocean.**
- How much of the earth is covered by the oceans? **About 71%.**

TAKING IT FURTHER

- How do the oceans affect the weather? **The oceans change temperature more slowly than land, so winds are generated near the ocean. Also, the heat energy in the ocean fuels many storms including hurricanes. Oceans are where most evaporation takes place so they ultimately generate most precipitation.**
- Why do some people say there is only one ocean? **All of the oceans are connected to each other so you could say there is only one ocean on earth.**
- Why was the Indian Ocean the first ocean to have established trade routes? **The monsoon winds blow steadily in one direction for half the year and then blow in the other direction the other half of the year. This made it easy for ships to sail to particular areas during certain times of the year.**

LESSON 24

COMPOSITION OF SEAWATER
ISN'T IT JUST WATER?

SUPPLY LIST

Dark construction paper   Salt   Paint brush   Water

BEGINNERS

- How does salt get into the ocean? **It is dissolved in rain water and carried by rivers to the ocean.**
- How does water get out of the ocean? **It evaporates.**
- What happens to the salt when water evaporates from the oceans? **It stays behind.**
- Why can fish and other plants live in the salty water? **God designed them to be able to live in the salty water.**

WHAT DID WE LEARN?

- What are the main elements found in the ocean besides water? **Salt, magnesium, and bromine.**
- How does salt get into the ocean? **Water flowing over land dissolves salt and other minerals then leaves them behind in the oceans when the water evaporates.**
- What is one gas that is dissolved in the ocean water? **Oxygen is the main gas; nitrogen, carbon dioxide, and other gases are present as well.**

TAKING IT FURTHER

- Why is there more oxygen near the surface of the ocean than in deeper parts? **Phytoplankton and other plants grow near the surface and produce oxygen that dissolves in the water. Also, some oxygen dissolves into the water from the air.**
- How does the saltiness of the ocean support the idea of a young earth? **If the earth were billions of years old, the amount of salt in the oceans would be much higher than it is today. The amount of salt in the ocean is consistent with an earth about 6,000 years old.**

LESSON 25 OCEAN CURRENTS

MOVING AROUND THE WORLD

SUPPLY LIST

2 small bottles or jars   Large glass bowl   Red and blue food coloring
Supplies for Challenge: World map from lesson 23

BEGINNERS

- What makes warmer water in the ocean move away from the equator? **Winds.**
- What happens to colder water in the ocean? **It sinks and moves from the poles toward the equator.**
- What is a river of moving water in the ocean called? **A current.**

WHAT DID WE LEARN?

- What is a surface ocean current? **A continuous movement of water in a particular direction on the surface of the ocean.**
- What are the main causes of surface currents? **Heating from the sun and movement by the wind.**
- How fast do surface currents usually move? **2–3 miles per hour.**
- What is a subsurface ocean current? **A continuous movement of water in a particular direction under the surface of the ocean.**

- What are the main causes of subsurface currents? **Differences in density of warmer and cooler water and differences in density of saltier and less salty water.**

TAKING IT FURTHER

- What climate changes do warm surface currents cause? **Coastal areas near warm currents tend to be warmer and have milder winters.**

- What climate changes do cool surface currents cause? **Coastal areas near cool currents tend to be drier than other areas, often resulting in deserts.**

- Why do warm surface currents move away from the equator while cooler currents move toward the equator? **The sun shines more intensely at the equator so the water is warmed more there than at the poles; the wind then moves this warm water away from the equator.**

LESSON 26

WAVES

GENTLY LAPPING THE SHORE

SUPPLY LIST

Small and large bottle   Tape   String   2 chairs

BEGINNERS

- What usually causes a wave to start? **Wind blowing across the surface of the water.**

- How does the water in a wave move? **In a circle—up and forward then down and back.**

- What is a tsunami? **A giant wave generated by an earthquake or a volcano.**

WHAT DID WE LEARN?

- How are waves generated? **Friction between the wind and the surface of the water picks up water and moves it a short distance. This adds energy to the surface of the ocean causing it to move in waves.**

- How far does a particular water molecule move when a wave is generated? **Only a short distance, perhaps a few feet at most.**

- What is the crest of a wave? **The crest is the highest part of the wave.**

- What is the trough of a wave? **The trough is the lowest part of the wave.**

- What are two ways to measure a wave? **Wave height—the difference between the crest and the trough, and wavelength—the distance between two crests.**

TAKING IT FURTHER

- Explain how a wave can move across the ocean without moving the water molecules across the ocean. **The individual molecules are moved a short distance by the wind. When they fall back down to the surface of the ocean they transfer their energy to other molecules that then move forward. Those molecules hit other molecules and so on until the wave dies or reaches the shore.**

- What kind of a path does an individual water molecule take in a wave? **It is lifted by the wind, moves forward, falls down and is pushed back by other molecules—so it travels in a small circular path.**

- Why does a wave get tall as it approaches the shore? **Friction causes the base of the wave to slow down when it hits the ocean floor. This pushes more water up, causing the wave to get taller and then break.**

- Why are tsunamis such dangerous waves? **A tsunami is a wave that travels very fast and has a tremendous amount of energy. As it reaches the shore, it causes large amounts of water to pile up so that a giant wall of water hits the shore causing massive flooding.**

LESSON 27 TIDES

THE HIGHS AND LOWS OF THE SEA

SUPPLY LIST

Copy of "Ocean Movements Word Search"

BEGINNERS

- What causes the level of the oceans to change? **The gravity from the moon.**
- What is a high tide? **When the level of the ocean is high; the water comes high up on the shore.**
- What is a low tide? **When the level of the ocean is low; the water does not come high up on the shore.**
- How many high tides are there each day? **Two.**

OCEAN MOVEMENTS WORD SEARCH

```
I P M C B E I Y D N E A P X Z
C B R G R A I F C E K P L U Y
U O E R I B L I M A N U S T W
R F W A V E L E N G T H T D Q
R H F V B R E A K E R F I E E
E K L I N J I E Y L O W W S R
N N E T L Y R E T V U C S C E
T D E Y S W H R I K G J G R V
X T Z Y W G O U S N H V F E L
M N H T I D E L N F T V N S O
V C K H N I H U E I R I P T B
R E D S D H I J D K L D E V D
C A F E H U F R I C T I O N N
I D I E C A F R U S B U S U X
V G I J K Y T S T R U N F Q O
```

WHAT DID WE LEARN?

- What is a high tide? **When the water level is the highest along a shore.**
- What causes the water level to change along the shore? **The gravitational pull of the moon and to a lesser extent the gravitational pull of the sun.**
- How often does a high or low tide occur each day? **There are two high tides and two low tides each day, approximately six hours apart.**

TAKING IT FURTHER

- Why does a spring tide only occur when there is a full moon or when there is a new moon? **This is the only time during the month when the sun is in a direct line with the earth and the moon, thus adding its gravitational pull to that of the moon.**

- Since the sun is so much larger than the moon, why doesn't it have a greater effect on the tides than the moon? **Because the moon is much closer than the sun: 240,000 miles (386,000 km) vs. 93 million miles (150 million km).**
- Where should you build your sandcastle if you don't want the water to knock it down? **Farther from the water than the highest point that the waves reach during high tide.**

LESSON 28

WAVE EROSION

WEARING DOWN THE SHORE

SUPPLY LIST

Paint roller pan   Sand   Empty plastic bottle
Supplies for Challenge: Copy of "Erosional Land Formations" worksheet

BEGINNERS

- How does water wear away the shoreline? **Waves pick up bits of sand and debris and move them out to deeper water. Water also breaks off bits of rock.**
- Do waves have to be big to cause changes to the shore? **No, even small waves cause changes.**

WHAT DID WE LEARN?

- What causes erosion along a beach? **Waves; large waves from storms and tsunamis cause the most damage, but everyday waves cause erosion as well.**
- What are some problems that can arise from wave erosion? **The changing shoreline can cause problems with buildings that are built too close to the shore. Also, sand that is moved from the shore can block bays and build up sand bars that block the movement of ships.**
- What features have been formed along the shore by the erosion from waves? **Sea caves, arches, and columns of stone.**

TAKING IT FURTHER

- Why don't shores completely erode if water is constantly pulling sand away from them? **Water is also bringing new sand and debris and depositing them as well.**
- How can you protect your building from the damaging effects of tsunamis and other storm-generated waves? **Build further from the shore.**

CHALLENGE: EROSIONAL LAND FORMATIONS WORKSHEET

1. **Spit**   2. **Hook**   3. **Barrier island**   4. **Bay barrier**

LESSON 29

ENERGY FROM THE OCEAN

MAKING IT WORK FOR US

SUPPLY LIST

The Magic School Bus on the Ocean Floor by Joanna Cole

BEGINNERS

- What are two forms of energy in the ocean? **Moving waves and heat.**

- How are people trying to use the energy from the ocean? **They are trying to use the movement of the waves to generate electricity. They are using the heat from the water to heat water in power plants.**

WHAT DID WE LEARN?

- What are three ways that people are using the ocean to generate electricity? **Tidal barriers, wave towers and wave buoys, and heat exchangers.**

- Have scientists given up on getting energy from the ocean because of the failures they have experienced? **No, they continue to do research and to look for better methods to harness the ocean's energy.**

TAKING IT FURTHER

- What can be done to improve the idea of the wave tower? **Build it stronger so it can use the force of the waves instead of being destroyed by it.**

- Why are tidal barriers used infrequently? **There are only a few places where there is a constant flow of water, and the barriers can damage the ecosystems.**

- Why do heat exchangers have to be built near the equator? **They rely on a difference in water temperature. The water that is hundreds of feet below the surface is cold no matter where you are, but the surface waters are consistently warm only in tropical areas.**

- Scientists hope to use the warm tropical waters to generate electricity. What natural weather phenomenon is fueled by these warm tropical waters? **Hurricanes, El Niño.**

QUIZ 6

OCEAN MOVEMENT

LESSONS 23–29

Fill in the blank with the correct term.

1. List the five oceans of the world. _**Pacific, Atlantic, Indian, Antarctic (or Southern), Arctic.**_

2. The _**monsoon**_ winds allowed trade routes to be established in the Indian Ocean.

3. The main mineral dissolved in seawater is _**salt**_.

4. There is more oxygen in the ocean near the surface because of _**algae**_ growing there.

5. The three main ways that the ocean moves are _**currents**_, _**tides**_, and _**waves**_.

6. Cold water is more _**dense**_ than warm water so it sinks.

7. Land near cold water currents tends to have weather that is **_dry and cold_**.

8. A body of warm water in the Pacific Ocean that greatly affects weather is **_El Niño_**.

9. The highest point of a wave is called the **_crest_**.

10. The lowest point of a wave is called the **_trough_**.

Mark each statement as either True or False.

11. **_F_** Water molecules are moved hundreds of miles across the ocean by waves.

12. **_T_** Friction between the air and the water causes waves to form.

13. **_F_** The highest part of a wave is called the trough.

14. **_T_** A tsunami is a very dangerous wave.

15. **_T_** Tides are a result of the gravitational pull of the moon.

16. **_T_** A rip current can pull a swimmer far out to sea.

17. **_F_** Erosion from waves is never harmful.

18. **_T_** Movement of the ocean is beneficial for all life on earth.

CHALLENGE QUESTIONS

Choose the best answer for each question or statement.

19. **_B_** What field of science began with the Challenger Expedition in 1872?

20. **_A_** How many volumes of information were published after the Challenger Expedition?

21. **_D_** Which is not a method of desalination?

22. **_A_** Where are the majority of desalination plants located?

23. **_C_** Major surface currents combine to form these five major circulations.

24. **_B_** Surface currents and prevailing winds rotate counterclockwise in the northern hemisphere due to this.

25. **_C_** What scale is used to describe wind and waves in the open ocean?

26. **_A_** What is the difference between high tide and low tide called?

27. **_D_** What is a whirlpool caused by changing tides called?

28. **_C_** What erosional land formation closes off the mouth of a bay?

SEA FLOOR

LESSON 30

SEA EXPLORATION

EXPLORING THE DEPTHS

SUPPLY LIST

Deck of playing cards

BEGINNERS

- How did most people explore the ocean in the past? **By holding their breath.**
- What invention allows divers to stay under the water for up to an hour? **The diving suit and air tank.**
- How do scientists study the deepest parts of the ocean? **In submersibles and with remotely operated vehicles.**

WHAT DID WE LEARN?

- What invention in the 1940s allowed divers to more freely explore the ocean? **The Aqua-Lung—a portable air tank.**
- How do oceanographers study the ocean today? **They scuba dive in relatively shallow water and they use submersibles and remotely operated vehicles to see what is in the deeper parts of the ocean.**
- What special equipment do submersibles have? **They are specially designed to withstand great water pressure. They have video cameras, manipulator arms, and storage containers for samples. They also have communication equipment.**

TAKING IT FURTHER

- Why does a submersible or ROV need headlights? **Below a few hundred feet (100 m), there is no sunlight and the water is very dark. Lights are needed so the scientists can see what is down there.**
- Why can't scuba divers go very deep in the ocean? **The water pressure is too great for their bodies.**
- How are submersibles similar to spacecraft? **They both provide protection to people from the surrounding environment by providing the right air pressure and by providing air to breathe. They both contain useful equipment that allows people to explore new areas.**

LESSON 31
GEOGRAPHY OF THE OCEAN FLOOR
MOUNTAINS AND VALLEYS

SUPPLY LIST

Empty aquarium or other glass case   Modeling clay

Supplies for Challenge: World map from lesson 23

BEGINNERS

- What is area of the ocean floor that slopes gently away from the shoreline? **The continental shelf.**
- What is the continental slope? **Where the ocean floor drops steeply.**
- What is the name of the relatively flat part of the ocean floor? **The abyssal plain.**
- What other features are found in the ocean floor? **Mountains, hills, and valleys.**

WHAT DID WE LEARN?

- What are the three areas of the ocean floor? **The continental shelf, the continental slope, and the abyssal plain.**
- What are some features of the abyssal plain? **There are relatively flat areas; there are seamounts, guyots, islands, and trenches.**
- What is a guyot? **An underwater mountain with a flat top.**

TAKING IT FURTHER

- What part of the ocean floor is most difficult to observe? **The trenches because they are so deep and have such great water pressure.**
- What do you think is the most likely cause of seamounts? **Volcanic activity is believed to cause nearly all seamounts.**

LESSON 32
OCEAN ZONES
VISITING THE DIFFERENT LEVELS

SUPPLY LIST

Copy of "Ocean Zones" worksheet   Crayons or colored pencils

Supplies for Challenge: Research materials on various sea creatures

BEGINNERS

- In what area are most plants and animals found? **In the sunlit zone.**
- What is the name of the area below the sunlit zone? **Twilight zone.**
- Which zones do not receive any sunlight? **Midnight, abyss, and trenches.**

Ocean Zones worksheet

- A. **Sunlit zone**   B. **Twilight zone**   C. **Midnight zone**   D. **Abyss**   E. **Trench**
- **Plants and animals: Accept reasonable answers—see lesson for examples.**

What did we learn?

- What are the five ocean zones? **Sunlit/euphotic zone, twilight/disphotic zone, midnight/aphotic zone, abyss, and trenches.**

- What zone has the most life? **The sunlit zone.**

- Where is the sunlit zone located? **Over the continental shelf, in the top 660 feet (300 m) of water.**

Taking it further

- Why is all plant life found in the sunlit zone? **Plants need sunlight to perform photosynthesis and grow, so they cannot live where no sunlight penetrates.**

- Why are so few animals found in the very deepest parts of the ocean? **The water pressure is too great for most animals. Those that can withstand the pressure must live where there is sufficient food.**

LESSON
33 Vents & Smokers

Underwater volcanoes?

Supply list

Paper   Colored pencils or markers

Beginners

- What is an ocean vent? **A place on the ocean floor where very hot water flows from below the earth's crust.**
- What mineral is found in this hot water? **Sulfur.**
- What kind of creature can survive on this sulfur? **Bacteria.**

What did we learn?

- What is a deep-sea vent? **An area on the sea floor where very hot water shoots up from below the surface of the ocean floor.**

- What provides the food source for the animals living near these vents? **A type of bacteria that thrives on the sulfur in the vent water.**

Taking it further

- Why were scientists so surprised to find an ecosystem thriving near the deep-sea vents? **They believed that all life in the sea depended on the plants growing in the sunlit zone, but this ecosystem gets its food supply from the bacteria that grow in the hot water.**

- Why can the water stay so hot near the vents without turning to steam? **The great pressure of the water at the depths in which the vents are found keeps the water in liquid form even at very high temperatures.**

LESSON 34

CORAL REEFS

ANIMAL-MADE ISLANDS

SUPPLY LIST

Modeling clay

BEGINNERS

- What is a coral? **A tiny animal shaped like an upside-down jellyfish.**
- How does a coral colony grow? **The corals build hard cups around their bodies and these cups are joined together to build a colony. As one dies a new one builds on top of the empty house.**
- Where do coral live? **Warm clear waters near the equator.**
- What other animals live near coral reefs? **Many fish, starfish, sea anemones, and sea urchins.**

WHAT DID WE LEARN?

- What is a coral? **A tiny animal that resembles an upside down jellyfish that lives in the ocean and secretes a hard cup around itself.**
- What is a coral reef? **A large collection of coral all growing together.**
- What are the three types of coral reefs? **Fringing reef, barrier reef, and atoll.**

TAKING IT FURTHER

- Why are coral reefs only found in relatively shallow ocean water? **The algae inside the coral require sunlight to make food.**
- Why might a coral reef be a hazard to ships? **A coral reef may not be visible from the surface but may be big enough to cause damage to the ship.**
- What could happen to a coral reef if the water became cloudy or too warm for the algae to survive? **The algae would die and the coral may eventually die as well.**

QUIZ 7

SEA FLOOR

LESSONS 30–34

1. Label the features of the ocean floor in the following diagram.
   A. **Continent**   E. **Abyssal plain**   B. **Continental shelf**   F. **Island**
   C. **Continental slope**   G. **Guyot**   D. **Seamount**   H. **Trench**

Below, label each ocean zone. Write each plant or animal from the list below next to the zone in which you are most likely to find it.

2. 0 to 660 feet is the _sunlit (or euphotic)_ zone. **Shark, algae, coral, jellyfish, seaweed**
3. 660 to 3,300 feet is the _twilight (or disphotic)_ zone. **Octopus, bioluminescent fish, sponges**
4. 3,300 to 13,200 feet is the _midnight (or aphotic)_ zone. **Tubeworms, anglerfish, sea spider**

5. 13,200 feet and deeper is called the _abyss_. **Sea lilies**

6. Very deep canyons are called _trenches_. **No plants or animals listed**

CHALLENGE QUESTIONS

Mark each statement as either True or False.

7. _F_ Astronauts primarily study conditions under the ocean.

8. _T_ Researchers can live in the Aquarius underwater lab for long periods of time.

9. _T_ Researchers in Aquarius must undergo a decompression period before surfacing.

10. _T_ Ocean trenches are found in subduction zones.

11. _F_ Ocean trenches and ridges are found in the same areas.

12. _T_ The Marianas Trench is the lowest place on Earth.

13. _F_ Most volcanic activity takes place on land.

14. _T_ Ocean vents are usually located near underwater volcanoes.

15. _F_ Coral reefs are proven to be hundreds of thousands of years old.

16. _T_ Coral reefs can grow very rapidly.

FINAL EXAM | OUR WEATHER & WATER

LESSONS 1–34

Fill in the blank with the correct term from below.

1. _Meteorology_ is the study of the earth's atmosphere.

2. _Climate_ is the average weather conditions in an area over a long period of time.

3. The earth's atmosphere is 78% _nitrogen_ and 21% _oxygen_.

4. The Genesis Flood set up environmental conditions just right for an _ice age_.

5. A _glacier_ can form when snow does not completely melt in the summer.

6. Water vapor that condenses in the air forms _clouds_.

7. Water that falls from the sky is called _precipitation_.

8. The _sun_ is responsible for most of the winds we experience on earth.

9. Hurricanes can only form near the _equator_.

10. The _computer_ is the most important piece of equipment for analyzing weather.

11. Weather fronts form where two _air masses_ meet.

Analyze the weather station model and fill in the blanks.

12. Temperature: **32°F**

13. Wind speed: **15 knots**

14. Wind direction: **North**

15. Precipitation: **Snow**

16. Cloud cover: **100%**

7. Air pressure: **1020.1 millibars**

Mark each statement as either True or False.

18. _F_ Relative humidity is the total amount of water vapor in the air.

19. _T_ Meteorologists use computers to help them forecast the weather.

20. _T_ The oceans play an important role in the weather.

21. _F_ El Niño is a wind in South America.

22. _T_ The ocean contains many minerals and gases in addition to water.

23. _T_ Ocean currents are sometimes a result of different amounts of salt in the water.

24. _T_ Energy from waves can be used to make electricity.

25. _F_ Waves are always helpful.

26. _F_ Tides are lower when the sun and the moon line up.

Match the term with its definition.

27. _F_ Most plants and animals are found in the twilight zone of the ocean.

28. _B_ Very deep valley in the ocean floor

29. _E_ Very hot water coming up through sea floor

30. _C_ Large collection of colonies of polyps

31. _H_ Vehicle for deep-sea exploration

32. _F_ Animal that can glow in the dark

33. _A_ Largest ocean on earth

34. _G_ Organism that produces most of the oxygen in the ocean

35. _D_ Strong current moving water from the shore to the open sea

36. _I_ Area where most plants and animals live in the ocean

CHALLENGE QUESTIONS

37. Use the following words to label the diagram of the atmosphere with the correct levels:

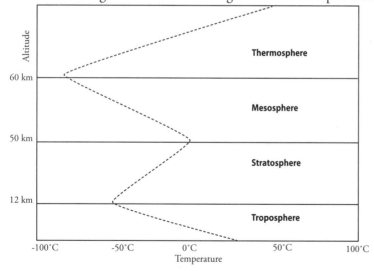

Short answer:

38. What are the four "ingredients" needed to make weather? **Earth, water, air, and sun.**

39. Explain how we get clues to what the climate was like in the past. **We get clues from fossils. The types of plants and animals found in an area can give us clues as to what the climate must have been like in order for those plants and animals to have lived there.**

40. List three kinds of fog. **Radiation, advection, steam, valley, upslope.**

41. What are two ways that acid rain can form? **Naturally—carbon dioxide in the atmosphere dissolves to create carbonic acid; chemically—sulfur and nitrogen compounds enter the air through pollution and dissolve in the water vapor to form sulfuric acid and nitric acid.**

42. The jet stream is most affected by the difference in temperature between which areas of the world? **Equator and the Poles.**

43. Name two kinds of radar that are used to detect severe weather. **Doppler, phased array.**

44. Explain how someone outside in the winter could feel more comfortable in a colder temperature than he or she does when the outside temperature is warmer. **The wind makes it feel colder because it increases the rate at which sweat evaporates, so if the wind is blowing more on a warmer day you could actually feel colder than if it blowing less on a colder day.**

45. What are two methods for desalinating ocean water. **Distillation, reverse osmosis.**

46. Do ocean ridges form where tectonic plates are moving toward each other or away from each other? **Away.**

LESSON

35

CONCLUSION

APPRECIATING OUR WEATHER AND WATER

SUPPLY LIST

Bible

APPENDICES

Resource Guide

Many of the following titles are available from Answers in Genesis (www.AnswersBookstore.com).

Our Universe

Suggested Books

Glow-In-The-Dark Nighttime Sky by Clint Hatchett—Easy-to-use star charts

Astronomy for Every Kid by Janice VanCleave—Many fun activities

The Astronomy Book by Jonathan Henry—a wealth of knowledge on subjects such as supernovas, red shift, facts about planets and much more

Astronomy and the Bible: Questions and Answers by Donald DeYoung—Answers to 110 questions on astronomy and the universe

Our Created Moon by Don DeYoung & John Whitcomb—Answers to 63 questions about the "lesser light"

Universe by Design by Danny Faulkner—Explores and explains the historical development of the science of astronomy from a creationist view

Taking Back Astronomy by Dr. Jason Lisle— Christian apologetics for astronomy

Suggested Videos

Newton's Workshop by Moody Institute— fun live action videos with Christian themes

Journey to the Edge of Creation by Moody Institute— beautiful film of universe

Creation Astronomy: Viewing the Universe Through Biblical Glasses by Dr. Jason Lisle (DVD)—Shows how the evidence of nature lines up perfectly with the clear teachings of Scripture

Created Cosmos: A Creation Museum Planetarium Show by Dr. Jason Lisle (DVD)—A visually stimulating tour of the universe underscoring its incomprehensible size and structure

Field Trip Ideas

- Creation Museum in Petersburg, Kentucky
- Observatory
- Space center or Space museum
- Planetarium
- Drive out to the country, away from city lights, to observe the night sky

Our Planet Earth

Suggested Books

Noah's Ark: A Feasibility Study by John Woodmorappe—An in-depth study that provides detailed answers to the major criticisms of Noah's Ark. (semi-technical)

The Geology Book by Dr. John D. Morris—Well illustrated, this book presents an accurate view of earth's natural history

The Fossils Book by Gary Parker— Uncovers the exciting story of fossils from a biblical view

The Young Earth by Dr. John D. Morris—Shows how true science supports a young age for the earth

In the Days of Noah by Earl & Bonnie Snellenberger—This spectacular book gives a wide-eyed look into what life must have been like 5,000 years ago

The True Story of Noah's Ark by Tom Dooley and Bill Looney—Spectacular artwork depicting the Ark, its interior, and the pre-Flood and post-Flood world

Grand Canyon: Monument to Catastrophe by Steven A. Austin, PhD—Geologist Dr. Steven Austin explains from a biblical standpoint how Grand Canyon was formed

Footprints in the Ash by Drs. John Morris and Steven Austin—Lavishly illustrated "picture book" that shares the full, explosive story of Mount St. Helens

Exploring Planet Earth by John Hudson Tiner—a biblical/historical view of the planet

Suggested Videos

Newton's Workshop by Moody Institute—Excellent Christian science series

Wonders of God's Creation by Moody Institute—3 DVD set includes Planet Earth, Animal Kingdom, and Human Life; beautiful photography

The Privileged Planet—Shows why the Earth is special and could not have happened by chance. (Intelligent Design)

Mount St. Helens by Institute for Creation Research—shows many exciting discoveries

Grand Canyon Monument to the Flood by ICR—tours Grand Canyon from creation perspective

Field Trip Ideas

- Creation Museum in Petersburg, Kentucky
- Museum with geology exhibits
- Hike in the hills or mountains
- Mining museum
- Visit a cave (one that is open to the public)

OUR WEATHER & WATER

Suggested Books

Weather and the Bible by Donald B. DeYoung—One hundred questions on weather-related topics are answered from the Christian perspective.

Life in the Great Ice Age by Michael and Beverly Oard—Learn what life was like during the Ice Age after the Flood in this colorful novel.

The Weather Book by Michael Oard—Provides a "big picture" view of weather and how it plays a role in our daily lives.

The Ocean Book by Frank Sherwin—You'll be amazed by what lies beneath the surface of the world's oceans!

The Magic School Bus on the Ocean Floor by Joanna Cole—fun and informative book

The Magic School Bus Inside a Hurricane by Joanna Cole—fun way to learn about storms

Frozen in Time by Michael Oard—explanation of woolly mammoth finds

Suggested Videos

Newton's Workshop by Moody Institute—Excellent Christian science series; several titles to choose from

Awesome Forces of God's Creation— 3 DVD set from Moody, includes Roaring Waters, Thundering Earth, and Whirling Winds

Field Trip Ideas

- Creation Museum in Petersburg, Kentucky
- Check if your area power company has wind generating equipment; set up a tour
- Beach (if one is nearby)
- Local weather station
- Visit a scuba diving school

CREATION SCIENCE RESOURCES

Answers Book for Kids Four volumes by Ken Ham with Cindy Malott—Answers children's frequently asked questions

The New Answers Book 1 & 2 by Ken Ham and others—Answers frequently asked questions

The Amazing Story of Creation by Duane T. Gish—Gives scientific evidence for the creation story

Creation Science by Felice Gerwitz and Jill Whitlock—Unit study focusing on creation

Creation: Facts of Life by Gary Parker—Comparison of the evidence for creation and evolution

The Young Earth by John D. Morris—Lots of facts disproving old-earth ideas

MASTER SUPPLY LIST

The following table lists all the supplies used for *God's Design for Heaven & Earth* activities. You will need to look up the individual lessons in the student book to obtain the specific details for the individual activities (such as quantity, color, etc.). The letter *c* denotes that the lesson number refers to the challenge activity. Common supplies such as colored pencils, construction paper, markers, scissors, tape, etc., are not listed.

Supplies needed (see lessons for details)	Our Universe	Our Planet Earth	Our Weather & Water
Alum (look in grocery spice aisle)		10	
Aluminum foil	20, 29		
Aquarium or other empty case	22		31
Baking soda		24	
Balloons	30		3
Bar of soap		28	
Basketball or volleyball	3, 14, 25		
Bathroom scale	27		
Bible	1, 18c, 35	35	35
Bottle with lid			22, 28
Building blocks	33	22	
Calculator	6c, 27		
Candle	22		2
Cardboard	11c	33	
Cereal bowls	23		
Chocolate chip cookies		17	
Chocolate chips		8, 8c, 25	
Chocolate syrup		25	
Clipboard	15c		
Collander		31c	
Cookie crumbs		25	
Cornstarch		11	
Cotton balls			11
Craft sticks		10	
Craft wire	34		
Cups (clear plastic or glass)	15, 19c, 21c, 22, 23c, 26		
Dirt/soil (from your yard)		29, 30, 30c, 31, 31c	
Display box (optional)		34	
Dry ice	22		10c
Duct tape			16, 22
Egg carton		15c	

Supplies needed (see lessons for details)	Our Universe	Our Planet Earth	Our Weather & Water
Epsom salt		13, 33	
Eye protection (goggles)		16	
Fine mesh strainer		31c	
Flashlight	3, 4, 6, 7, 14, 15c, 16, 19c, 21c 26, 35		
Flour	10		12
Food coloring	26	24	22, 25
Glitter	9		
Global warming articles			8
Globe of the earth	21		
Gloves	22	7, 7c	10c
Golf ball	2, 10		
Graham crakers		19c	
Graph paper	20c		2c, 21c
Gumballs		8	
Hairdryer	19		
Hammer		16	
House plant			6
Ice	15, 19	6	10
Ice cream		25	
Index card	12c, 19c, 25c, 34c		
Jar with lid		3, 7c, 8	2, 3c, 10, 19, 25, 26, 28
Lamp			4
Liquid dish soap	22		
Magnet	28		
Magnifying glass	4, 19c	10c, 16, 31	
Marbles	10, 23		
Marshmallows (large)		8	
Masking tape	3, 18	1, 16	3, 4, 14, 19, 26
Matches	22		2, 11c
Metal clothes hanger			14
Milk	21c		
Milk carton (empty, ½-gallon)		7	
Mirror	4, 12, 33		6
Model rocket and launch pad (optional)	29		
Modeling clay	3c, 20c, 25c, 29	12, 22c, 28, 32	2, 22, 29, 31, 34
Motorcycle helmet with face plate, or bike helmet (optional)	33		
Newspaper		7c, 21, 24, 31c	1, 5, 21
Nut and bolt	33		

Supplies needed (see lessons for details)	Our Universe	Our Planet Earth	Our Weather & Water
Orange (fruit)	21		
Paint	25, 34	11	
Paint roller pan			28
Paper cups		10, 11c, 30c, 31c, 33	
Peanut butter (creamy) or frosting		19c	
Pencils (wooden)	25c		
Petroleum jelly		12	
pH testing paper (optional)			12c
Piece of cloth			15, 18
Ping-pong ball	2, 25		
Plaster of Paris		11c, 12	
Plastic bottle (empty, 2-liter)		24	11c, 13, 16, 22, 26
Plastic grocery bag			3c
Plastic lid or dish	28		
Plastic tornado tube (optional but recommended)			16
Plastic tubing (clear)			22
Plastic wrap	20		
Plastic zipper bag		7c, 8c, 28c	10
Playing cards			30
Poster board/tagboard	9, 28, 29	34	22
Potting soil		31	
Prism (optional)	12		
Protractor	25c		
Real chalk (made from limestone, not sidewalk chalk) or limestone rock		28	
Reflector (like from a bicycle)	16		
Rock and mineral guide		10c, 11c, 14c, 16, 34	
Rock and mineral samples		9c, 10c, 11c, 14c, 15c, 16, 34	
Rolling pin		23	
Rubber band			18
Ruler	6, 20c		
Salt	10		24
Sand		11	19, 28
Shaved ice (or fresh snow if available)		14	
Shoe box	20, 20c	23	10c
Short ruler (6-inch)			22
Sidewalk chalk	13		
Sling psychrometer (optional)			18
Soft drink (unopened can)		25c	

Supplies needed (see lessons for details)	Our Universe	Our Planet Earth	Our Weather & Water
Sponges		13, 21c	
Star chart	5		
Steel BBs	28		
Steel wool without soap		28c	
Stop watch		31c	
Straw	30	27, 28	22
String	11c, 20c, 26c, 30	1, 33	3, 4, 12, 22, 26
Stuffed animal			15
Styrofoam balls	9, 29, 34		
Styrofoam rings	34		
Taffy or other soft candy		14	
Tea bag	23c		
Telescope (optional)	4, 16c		
Tennis ball	14	1	
The Magic School Bus on the Ocean Floor			29
Thermometer	15, 20		18
Thumb tacks	11c		
Toothpicks		8, 17	
Tops (spinning toys)	18		
Towel	19		
Toy boat		6	
Toy houses, cars, etc.	10		
Tracing paper		19	
Trash bag (large)			14
Tripod	3c		
Turntable (swivel chair, stool, Lazy Susan, etc.)	3c		
Unglazed ceramic tile		16	
Vinegar		24, 28	
Washer	20c, 26c		
Waxed paper	32	8, 14, 19c	
Weather station (optional)			22
Winter clothes	33		
Wooden stick (small, skewer-like)			22
World atlas/map	21	5c, 20c, 24c	5, 23
Yard stick/meter stick	6, 12c		3

WORKS CITED

OUR UNIVERSE

"About Foucault Pendulums and How They Prove the Earth Rotates!" http://www.calacademy.org/products/pendulum.

"About NASA." http://www.nasa.gov/about/highlights/index.html.

Arty Facts Space & Art Activities. Ed. Ellen Rodger. New York: Crabtree Publishing Company, 2002.

"Astronauts May Commute in New Vehicle." *Windsor Tribune*. 1 September 2003: A6.

Behrens, June. *Sally Ride, Astronaut An American First*. Chicago: Children's Press, 1984.

Bonnet, Bob, and Dan Keen. Flight,Space & Astronomy. New York: Sterling Publishing, 1997.

Bourgeois, Paulette. *The Sun*. Buffalo: Kids Can Press, Ltd., 1997.

Caprara, Giovanni. *Living in Space*. Milan: Firefly Books, 2000.

"Civilian Space Travel." http://www.kidsastronomy.com/civilian_space_travel.

Cole, Michael D. *Hubble Space Telescope Exploring the Universe*. Springfield: Enslow Publishers, Inc., 1999.

Cole, Michael D. *NASA Space Vehicles*. Berkley Heights: Enslow Publishers, Inc., 2000.

"Deep Impact." http:// deepimpact.umd.edu.

DeYoung, Donald. *Astronomy and the Bible*. Grand Rapids: Baker Book House, 1989.

Dickinson, Terrance. *Exploring the Night Sky*. Toronto: Camden House, 1987.

"Finding the Size of the Sun and the Moon." http://cse.ssl.berkeley.edu/AtHomeAstronomy/activity_03.html

"First Flight of SpaceShipOne Into Space." http://www.richard-seaman.com/Aircraft/AirShows/SpaceShipOne2004/.

Gifford, Clive. *The Kingfisher Facts and Records Book of Space*. New York: Kingfisher, 2001.

Hatchett, Clint. *The Glow-in-the-Dark Night Sky Book*. New York: Random House, 1988.

Henry, Jonathan. *The Astronomy Book*. Green Forest: Master Books, 2005.

Hitt, Robert, Jr. *The Sun's Family*. Danbury: Grolier Educational, 1998. Vol. 1 of *Outer Space*.

"James Webb Space Telescope." http://ngst.gsfc.nasa.gov.

Kerrod, Robin. *The Moon*. Minneapolis: Lerner Publications Co., 2000.

"Jupiter's New Red Spot." http://science.nasa.gov/headlines/y2006/02mar_red.

"Mauna Kea Telescopes." http://www.ifa.hawaii.edu/mko/telescope_table.htm.

Meyers, Robert. "Giant Telescopes Combine to Form World's Largest." http://www.space.com/scienceastronomy/astronomy.

Mulfinger, George, and Donald E. Snyder. *Earth Science for Christian Schools*. Greenville: Bob Jones University Press, 1992.

"NASA." http:// www.nasa.gov. National Aeronautics and Space Administration. *Spinoffs*. Washington, DC: NASA, 1988.

National Aeronautics and Space Administration. *The Amazing Hubble Space Telescope*. John F. Kennedy Space Center: NASA, 1986.

"New Horizons." http://www.nasa.gov/mission_pages/newhorizons/main/.

"Prepared for the Mission: A Tribute to Rick Husband." *Homeschooling Today*. Mar/Apr 2003: 30–33.

Rau, Dana M. *Jupiter*. Minneapolis: Compass Point Books, 2002.

Rau, Dana M. *Mars*. Minneapolis: Compass Point Books, 2002.

"Raymond Orteig—$25,000 Prize." http://www.charles-lindbergh.com/plane/orteig.asp.

Rau, Dana M. *Mercury*. Minneapolis: Compass Point Books, 2002.

Rau, Dana M. *Neptune*. Minneapolis: Compass Point Books, 2003.

Rau, Dana M. *Pluto*. Minneapolis: Compass Point Books, 2003.

Rau, Dana M. *Saturn*. Minneapolis: Compass Point Books, 2003.

Rau, Dana M. *Uranus*. Minneapolis: Compass Point Books, 2003.

Rau, Dana M. *Venus*. Minneapolis: Compass Point Books, 2002.

"Saturn Probe Sights Mystery Moon." http://news.bbc.co.uk/1/hi/sci/tech/3633297.stm.

Simon, Seymour. *Our Solar System*. New York: Morrow Junior Books, 1992.

"Saturn's Rings." http://saturn.jpl.nasa.gov/science/index.cfm?PageI.

"Space Camp." http:// www.spacecamp.com.

Spangenburg, Ray, and Kit Moser. *Mercury*. New York: Franklin Watts, 2001.

Spangenburg, Ray, and Kit Moser. *Venus*. New York: Franklin Watts, 2001.

Spence, M. *Solar Power*. New York: Gloucester Press, 1982.

"Sunspots." http://www.exploratorium.edu/sunspots/research7.html.

VanCleave, Janice. *Astronomy for Every Kid*. New York: John Wiley & Sons, Inc., 1991.

VanCleave, Janice. *Solar System*. New York: John Wiley& Sons, 2000.

"The Vision for Space Exploration." http://www.nasa.gov/missions/solarsystem/explore_main_old.html.

"Were Stars Created?" http://www.answersingenesis.org/creation/v18/i2/stars.asp.

Our Planet Earth

Science Encyclopedia. Ed. Susan McKeever. London: DK Publishing, 1998.

Blobaum, Cindy. *Geology Rocks!* Charlotte: Williamson Publishing, 1999.

DeYoung, Donald. *Thousands...Not Billions*. Green Forest: Master Books, 2005.

Gallant, Roy A. *Dance of Continents*. New York: Benchmark Books, 2000.

Gallant, Roy A. *Geysers—When Earth Roars*. New York: Franklin Watts, 1997.

Gallant, Roy A. *Limestone Caves*. New York: Franklin Watts, 1998.

"Geology:The Active Earth." *Nature Scope*. Feb 1988: 1–20.

Gerwitz, Felice, and Jill Whitlock. *Creation Geology*. Fort Meyers: Media Angels, 1997.

"The Geysers." http://www.geysers.com/kids.htm.

Ham, Ken, et al. *The Answers Book*. El Cajon: Master Books - Creation Science Foundation Ltd., 1990.

Harrison, David L. *Volcanoes—Nature's Incredible Fireworks*. Honesdale: Boyds Mills Press, 2002.

Mandia, Scott A. "The Little Ice Age in Europe." http://www2.sunysuffolk.edu/mandias/lia/little_ice_age.html.

Mannes, Judy. "Volcanoes." *Kids Discover*. 1999: 1–20.

"The Mineral Native Selenium." http://mineral.galleries.com/minerals/elements/selenium/selenium.htm.

"Mineralogy 4 Kids." http://www.minsocam.org/MSA/K12/K_12.html.

Morris, John D., PhD. *The Young Earth*. Colorado Springs: Master Books, Creation Life Publishers, Inc., 1994.

Mulfinger, Jr., George, M.S., and Donald E. Snyder, M.Ed. *Earth Science for Christian Schools*. 2nd ed. Greenville: Bob Jones University Press, 1995.

"Native Element." http://www.britannica.com/EBchecked/topic/405982/native-element.

"New Mt. St. Helens Sensors Will Take Its Pulse." http://community.seattletimes.nwsource.com/archive/?date=20060924&slug=sthelens24.

Oard, Michael. "Global Warming." http://www.answersingenesis.org/articles/am/v1/n2/global-warming.

Price, Sean. "Rocks." *Kids Discover*. April 2002: 1–20.

"Creation Quotes." http://www.answersingenesis.org/home/area/tools/quotes.asp.

Ricciuti, Edward, and Margaret W. Carruthers. *First Field Guide Rocks and Minerals*. New York: Scholastic Inc., 1998.

"Rock Glacier." http://geology.about.com/library/bl/images/blrockglacier.htm.

"Rock Glaciers: An Introduction with Examples from the Austrian Alps." http://www.uibk.ac.at/projects/rock-glacier/rockglacier_intro.html.

Rodrigue, Dr. "Lecture : Composition of the Earth's Crust." http://www.csulb.edu/~rodrigue/geog140/lectures/crustmaterials.html.

Su, Adrienne. "Earthquakes." *Kids Discover*. 1999: 1–20.

Vail, Tom. *Grand Canyon: a Different View*. Green Forest: Master Books, 2005.

VanCleave, Janice. *A+ Projects in Earth Science*. New York: John Wiley & Sons, 1999.

VanCleave, Janice. *Earth Science for Every Kid*. New York: John Wiley & Sons, 1991.

VanRose, Susanna. *Volcano and Earthquake*. New York: Eyewitness Books, 1992.

Woolley, Alan. *Spotter's Guide to Rocks & Minerals*. London: Usborne Publishing Ltd, 2000.

Our Weather & Water

"Acid Rain." http://www.epa.gov/acidrain/index.html.

Ardley, Neil. *The Science Book of Weather*. San Diego: Gulliver Books, 1992.

"Ashkelon Desalination Plane, Seawater Reverse Osmosis (SWRO) Plant, Israel." http://www.water-technology.net/projects/israel/.

"Benjamin Franklin." http://web.lemoyne.edu/~giunta/franklin.html.

Brice, Tim. "Heat Index." http://www.srh.noaa.gov/elp/wxcalc/heatindex.shtml.

"California's Rocky Intertidal Zones." http://ceres.ca.gov/ceres/calweb/coastal/rocky.html.

Cobb, Allan B. *Weather Observation Satellites*. New York: Rosen Publishing Group, 2003.

"Colorado Remembers Big Thompson Canyon Flash Flood of 1976." http://www.noaanews.noaa.gov/stories/s688.htm.

Conjecture Corp. "What is the Jet Stream?" http://www.wisegeek.com/what-is-the-jet-stream.htm.

Coutsoukis, Photius. "Russian Climate." http://www.photius.com/countries/russia/climate/russia_climate_climate.html.

Daly, John L. "The El Niño Southern Oscillation." http://www.john-daly.com/elnino.htm.

Demarest, Chris L. *Hurricane Hunters! Rides on the Storm*. New York: Margaret K. McElderry Books, 2006

DeYoung, Donald B. *Weather & the Bible*. Grand Rapids: Baker Book House, 1996.

"El Niño Warm Water Pool Decreasing." http://visibleearth.nasa.gov/view_rec.php?id=542.

Fleisher, Paul. *Coral Reef*. New York: Benchmark Books, 1998.

"Fog." http://www.bbc.co.uk/weather/features/understanding/fog.shtml.

Fredericks, Anthony D. *Exploring the Oceans—Science Activities for Kids*. Golden: Fulcrum Resources, 1998.

Gardiner, Brian. *Energy Demands*. London: Gloucester Press, 1990.

Gardner, Robert. *Science Project Ideas About Rain*. Berkely Heights: Enslow Publishers, Inc., 1997.

Gibbons, Gail. *Exploring the Deep, Dark Sea*. Boston: Little, Brown and Company, 1999.

Gray, Susan H. *Coral Reefs*. Minneapolis: Compass Point Books, 2001.

Harper, Suzanne. *Clouds: From Mares Tails to Thunderheads*. New York: Franklin Watts, 1997.

Haslam, Andrew, and Barbara Taylor. *Make It Work Weather*. Chicago: World Book, 1997.

"Intertidal Zones." http://neptune.spaceports.com/~marine/life.html.

Jones, Lorraine. *Super Science Projects About Weather and Naturals Forces*. New York: Rosen Central, 2000.

"Joseph Priestly, The King of Serendipity." http://home.nycap.rr.com/useless/priestly/priestly.html.

Kahl, Jonathan D. *Storm Warning: Tornadoes and Hurricanes*. Minneapolis: Lerner Publications Co., 1993

Lambert, David. *Weather*. New York: Franklin Watts, 1983.

Low, Anne Marie. "Dust Bowl Diary." http://chnm.gmu.edu.

Meltzer, Milton. *Benjamin Franklin The New American*. New York: Franklin Watts, 1988.

Mulfinger, George, and Donald E. Snyder. *Earth Science for Christian Schools*. Greenville: Bob Jones University Press, 1995.

National Wildlife Federation. *Wild About Weather*. Philadelphia: Chelsea House Publishers, 1997.

"New Detection System Listens for Tornadoes." *Windsor Tribune*. 27 May 2003.

Oard, Michael. "Human-caused Global Warming Slight So Far." http://www.answersingenesis.org/articles/aid/v1/n1/human-caused-global-warming.

Oard, Michael, and Beverly Oard. *Life in the Great Ice Age*. Colorado Springs: Master Books, 1993.

Oard, Michael. *The Weather Book*. Green Forest: Master Books, 2000.

"Ocean Currents." http://seawifs.gsfc.nasa.gov/OCEAN_PLANET/HTML/oceanography_currents_1.html.

"Ocean Exploration and Undersea Research Hydrothermal Vents." http://www.research.noaa.gov/oceans/t_vents.html.

Oxlade, Chris. *Weather*. Austin: Raintree Steck-Vaughn, 1999.

"Quick Bits of 'L'." *Tidbits*. 8 October 2003: 2.

"Saltwater Desalination in California." http://www.coastal.ca.gov/desalrpt/dchap1.html.

Sands, Stella. "Tornadoes." *Kids Discover*. June/July 1996: 1–20.

Scher, Linda. "Hurricanes." *Kids Discover*. June 2002: 1–20.

Seibert, Patricia. *Discovering El Nino*. Brookfield: Millbrook Press, 1999.

"Sheele, Karl Wilhelm." http://www.1911encyclopedia.org/Karl_Wilhelm_Scheele.

Sherwin, Frank. *The Ocean Book*. Green Forest: Master Books, 2006.

Silverstein, Alvin, and others. *Weather and Climate*. Brookfield: Twenty-First Century Books, 1998.

Simon, Seymour. *Tornadoes*. New York: Morrow Junior Books, 1999.

Suplee, Curt. "El Nino/La Nina Nature's Vicious Cycle." www.nationalgeographic.com.

"Surviving the Dust Bowl." http://www.pbs.org/wgbh/amex/dustbowl.

"Take the 'A' Train." http://www.spacetoday.org/Satellites/TerraAqua.

Talbot, Frank H. *Under the Sea*. New York: Barnes & Nobel Books, 2003.

"The Tsunami Story." http://www.tsunami.noaa.gov/tsunami_story.html.

Waters, John F. *Deep-Sea Vents Living Worlds Without Sun*. Dutton: Cobblehill Books, 1994.

"Weather Radar." http://www.nssl.noaa.gov/research/radar.

"What is an El Niño?" http://www.pmel.noaa.gov/tao/elnino/el-nino-story.html.

Williams, Jack. "Doppler Radar is a Key Forecasting Tool." http://www.usatoday.com/weather/wdoppler.htm.

Wilmsen, Emily. "Colorado State Goes Into Orbit with CloudSat." CSU Alumni. Fall 2006: 4–5.